# Overcoming Narcissistic Abuse

Your F.R.E.E Guide to Empowering Yourself, Breaking Free From Abuse, Achieving Peace, and Finding Closure

Dr. Patricia Natpikia

© **Copyright 2022 - All rights reserved.**

The content contained within this book may not be reproduced, duplicated or transmitted without direct written permission from the author or the publisher.

Under no circumstances will any blame or legal responsibility be held against the publisher, or author, for any damages, reparation, or monetary loss due to the information contained within this book, either directly or indirectly.

Legal Notice:

This book is copyright protected. It is only for personal use. You cannot amend, distribute, sell, use, quote or paraphrase any part, or the content within this book, without the consent of the author or publisher.

Disclaimer Notice:

Please note the information contained within this document is for educational and entertainment purposes only. All effort has been executed to present accurate, up to date, reliable, complete information. No warranties of any kind are declared or implied. Readers acknowledge that the author is not engaged in the rendering of legal, financial, medical or professional advice. The content within this book has been derived from various sources. Please consult a licensed professional before attempting any techniques outlined in this book.

By reading this document, the reader agrees that under no circumstances is the author responsible for any losses, direct or indirect, that are incurred as a result of the use of the information contained within this document, including, but not limited to, errors, omissions, or inaccuracies.

# Table of Contents

**INTRODUCTION** ........................................................................... 1
   STEPPING OUT OF THE SHADOWS .............................................. 2
      *What This Journey Entails* .................................................. 4
      *The Benefits of This Journey* ............................................. 4
      *Let's Get Going* ................................................................. 6

**CHAPTER 1: THE STORY OF NARCISSISM** ................................. 7
   UNDERSTANDING NARCISSISM ...................................................... 9
      *Narcissistic Personality Disorder: Signs, Symptoms, and Causes* ............................................................................. 10
      *Narcissistic Personality Disorder: Traits and Characteristics* ................................................................................ 14
      *Narcissistic Personality Disorder: The Side Effects* .......... 17

**CHAPTER 2: THE MYTHS OF NARCISSISTIC ABUSE** ................ 21
   DEBUNKING MISCONCEPTIONS REGARDING NARCISSISTIC ABUSE ...... 23
      *Debunked Myth #1: It's Not Abuse if You Don't Have Scars* .................................................................................. 25
      *Debunked Myth #2: Don't Be Fooled by Picture Perfect Facades* ............................................................................. 25
      *Debunked Myth #3: All Mental Illnesses Are Diagnosed and Treated* ...................................................................... 26
      *Debunked Myth #4: It Won't Happen Again* .................. 28
      *Debunked Myth #5: Passes for Difficult Childhoods* ....... 29
      *Debunked Myth #6: Forgiveness for Being Nice* ............. 30
      *Debunked Myth #7: Other People Experience Abuse, Not Me* ..................................................................................... 31
      *Debunked Myth #8: Confidence Is an Olympic Sport* ...... 32

**CHAPTER 3: TYPES OF NARCISSISTIC ABUSE** .......................... 35
   EMOTIONAL ABUSE ................................................................. 37

  *Under the Microscope: Identifying Emotional Abuse* ...... 39
  *Under the Microscope: The Side Effects of Emotional Abuse* ................................................................ 42
 VERBAL ABUSE ................................................................ 44
  *Under the Microscope: Identifying Verbal Abuse*........... 47
  *Under the Microscope: The Side Effects of Verbal Abuse* 51
 PHYSICAL ABUSE ............................................................. 54
  *Under the Microscope: Identifying Physical Abuse* ......... 57
  *Under the Microscope: The Side Effects of Physical Abuse* ................................................................................ 59

## CHAPTER 4: ALL ABOUT GASLIGHTING ................................. 63

 UNDERSTANDING GASLIGHTING ................................................. 65
  *The Origin of Gaslighting*................................................. 66
  *Under the Microscope: Identifying the Signs of Gaslighting* ................................................................................ 67
 GASLIGHTING: THE GUIDED PROCESS YOUR NARCISSISTIC ABUSER DOESN'T WANT YOU TO KNOW ................................................. 72
  *Stage One: Lies and Exaggerations*................................. 73
  *Stage Two: Constant Repetition* ..................................... 74
  *Stage Three: Chernobyl Gaslighting Event*....................... 74
  *Stage Four: Mentally Defeating the Victim* ..................... 75
  *Stage Five: Codependency Relationships*......................... 76
  *Stage Six: Fool's Paradise* ................................................ 76
  *Stage Seven: Ultimate Authority*...................................... 77
  *The Results of Being a Victim of Gaslighting* .................. 78

## CHAPTER 5: FINDING YOUR INNER PEACE ............................. 83

 IT'S ALL ABOUT PEACE ........................................................... 85
  *Finding Peace Between the Layers of Fear* ..................... 86
 BABY STEPS TOWARDS INNER PEACE: TIPS AND TOOLS ................... 88
  *Adopting Acceptance on Your Journey to Inner Peace* .... 89
  *Educate Yourself on Your Journey to Inner Peace* .......... 90
  *Journaling*....................................................................... 95
  *Consider Having a Support System* ................................ 97

## CHAPTER 6: REVERING IN ULTIMATE FREEDOM .................. 101

 EMBRACING YOUR LONG-AWAITED FREEDOM ............................ 102

*The Essence of Freedom* ............................................. 103
*Prison Break: The Plan* ............................................. 104
*Prison Break: The Execution* ..................................... 109

**CHAPTER 7: EXHIBITING A WAVE OF SELF-TRUST** ............... 113

TAKING BACK WHAT BELONGS TO YOU ..................................... 115
*No More Dangling Carrots: Re-Claiming Me* ............... 116
*Show Yourself Some Mercy and Kindness* .................... 120
*Learning the Act of Self-Love and Self-Appreciation* ..... 121

**CHAPTER 8: EXPERIENCING THE FINAL CLOSURE** ................. 125

ALL OBSTACLES OUT OF THE WAY: IMPENDING CLOSURE OF A RELATIONSHIP .................................................................. 127
*Oh No, You Aren't Going Anywhere—Regards, Your Narcissist* ............................................................... 128
*Spine Straight, Shoulders Square, Turn, and Walk Away* ............................................................... 130
*Mourn the Demise of Your Relationship* ..................... 133
*The Final Closure: Crossing the Last Hurdle* ................. 137

**CONCLUSION** ........................................................ 141

THANK YOU ............................................................. 142

**REFERENCES** ........................................................ 143

**Trigger Warning:**

This book may contain text that could be upsetting to readers who have been affected by trauma associated with physical, mental, or emotional abuse.

**Medical Disclaimer:**

Please consult a medical professional should you require assistance regarding any medication, treatment plans, or psychological diagnosis.

# Introduction

*Narcissism is voluntary blindness, an agreement not to look beneath the surface.* –Sam Keen

I would like to invite you to embark on this journey of overcoming narcissistic abuse. This book is going to offer you a place where you will be safe from bullying, condemnation, and judgment. This journey is all about you, your feelings, and the steps you can take to free yourself from the clutches of those who don't want you to succeed in life. I want to show you that you are worthy of the spotlight that shines on you, and that you have every right to be the person you were born to be. I would like to ask you a couple of questions before we continue on this journey. I ask the questions that you are too afraid to ask. You know what your answers are going to be. You may be afraid to acknowledge the answers because they will only confirm what you already suspect.

Answer the following questions as truthfully as you can. I would like you to know that you are in a safe place. You are in control at all times, and you don't have to be afraid. While you are with me, in this book, your safety will not be compromised.

Is your partner jealous of the attention you receive from others?

Does your partner cut you off mid-sentence during a conversation?

Does your partner believe that they are always right, even when they are not?

Does your partner command the spotlight at business, family, or social events?

Is your partner showering you with affection in front of others but belittles you behind closed doors?

If you have nodded in answer, then you may be the victim of a narcissistic relationship. You are not the first, and you most definitely will not be the last person to find yourself in such a relationship. Most people have been in narcissistic relationships for so long that they don't even realize it. Others may have experienced hints of narcissistic behavior in the early stages of their relationships.

## Stepping Out of the Shadows

Would you believe me if I told you that I know how you are feeling? I've been in a similar position. I was pushed into the shadows where I was isolated. I felt as if I had entered another dimension where I didn't recognize my partner. I was trapped in the quicksand of my life. I felt both helpless and hopeless because I didn't know what to do. My knight in shining armor became my worst nightmare. Everything that happened was my fault, and I believed it. Everything my partner said was maliciously twisted around to make me look like the one with the problem. My partner was the master of manipulation. I reached a stage in my life where I knew that this wasn't the life I was meant to be part of. I stepped out of the shadows. I reclaimed and rebuilt my life. I can share my experience with everyone else because I know what it is like to be placed in a glass cage, in the shadows, on display.

I found the courage, deep within my soul, to claim back my life. I smashed that glass cage that had been holding me captive for far too long. I found my freedom, my island in the sun, where I can absorb all the attention and love that I am worthy of. This book is about equipping you with all the tools that you will need to find your way to the peace that your mind, body, and soul deserve. I am going to share all the tips and tricks that I used to get me where I am today. You are going to learn how to break the bonds of your past, take control of your present, and shape your future. Don't ever let anyone tell you that you don't deserve the best. This world is big enough for you to shine brightly. You are not going to return to the shadows of doubt, bullying, and condemnation. You don't have to stand up to those who don't treat you with the respect you deserve.

## *What This Journey Entails*

We are going to start this journey by taking a step back in time. You may feel intimidated, but no one can hurt you here. We need to take a step back in time to find the healing that is necessary so that we can move forward. You won't know what to fix if you can't identify the cracks. The first couple of chapters are going to be about the discovery surrounding the concept of narcissism and the abuse associated with it. You are going to learn about the various types of narcissistic attributes that have been part of your life, including identifying the different traits associated with partners.

You may be feeling overwhelmed at the thought of what the first couple of chapters holds for you. Your heart may be threatening to escape from your chest. The blood may be pooled in your feet. I am giving you a preview of what is waiting for you, so that you don't feel as if you have been ambushed. You may recall that I promised you that you would be safe in this book. No one can hurt you here. This is your little life raft, and when you are ready, you can jump onto the yacht and sail off into the sunset. And, let me tell you, the sunset is worth working through the past.

## *The Benefits of This Journey*

You are more resilient and braver than what you give yourself credit for. You are filled with determination to fight your way back from the clutches of domination. You are admired by those who never thought it was possible to claim back what was stolen from you—the light in your eyes. I know that you have walked through fields of thorns to get to where you are now, but at the end of it all, you are the champion of your world. You are stronger than ever because you have reclaimed your rightful position in the spotlight. It doesn't matter if you have not yet overcome your narcissistic relationship. The fact that you are here, reading this, already makes you a superstar.

You knew, when you chose this book, that it was going to be a difficult journey. Some may even say that this is an impossible journey. Taking a step back in time is something that is needed so that you can start the healing process. When you are done taking a step back in time, you are in for a life lesson that you may wish you had on the day you started understanding what life was all about. The rest of the book is going to be all about equipping you with a diamond-studded, platinum-encrusted toolkit that is going to help you shape and mold the future you rightfully deserve. I am going to ensure that the stars sparkle for you again.

Your toolkit will include the F.R.E.E. method, which is going to help you overcome and reign supreme over the narcissistic abuse you have endured. You are going to regain your independence as you grow from strength to strength. The light that will be radiating from you is going to show everyone how you have healed from the toxic relationship that held you captive. You are going to earn yourself a bright, shining star that is going to prove to others that hope does exist. You are going to be an inspiration to others who have been too afraid to venture beyond the walls of their glass cases.

## *Let's Get Going*

Are you here to help a friend who can't see what their relationship entails? Are you the person who has seen, collected all the bright red narcissistic flags, and headed out the door? Have you been in the narcissistic pool, worn the t-shirts, burned them all, and are now in a position to help others? It doesn't matter where you are at this stage of your journey through life. The most important part of this journey is that you are stronger than you were. You want to be empowered so that you can be a beacon of strength to other, unsuspecting victims. I cannot stress it enough, but you have a right to be happy, to smile, be uplifted, and be heard.

For your convenience, please ensure that you are wearing your most comfortable sweats or pajamas. Fluffy socks and a minky blanket are optional and season-dependent. Ensure that you have your Stanley cup filled with ice water or your favorite beverage of choice—you need to stay hydrated. Please make sure that your snack basket is filled with all your favorite treats so that you don't have to move unless you absolutely have to. Remember that you are entering a safe space, where you will be protected and no one can hurt you in this book. Let's go…

# Chapter 1:

# The Story of Narcissism

I believed that the relationship I had with my narcissistic partner was normal. I did everything in my power to keep my partner happy. I showered them with affection, attention, respect, and whatever they needed to be happy. I was slightly late showing up to the "reciprocating of needs" party. Alarm bells started going off in my head when I did eventually show up. I would sidle up closer, and my partner would take a very slight and subtle step away from me. I would reach out to hold their hand, and they would pull away. I would want to snuggle on the couch while we watched a movie, but my partner would move to another seat. That is when it dawned on me that it was all about them. The terms of our relationship were all about what *they* wanted and demanded. Unfortunately, the terms and conditions of our relationship excluded *me* and *my* needs. I wasn't privy to the same terms because I was not deemed worthy of attention, affection, or respect.

Family, social, and work events were interesting. My partner was charming in front of an audience. Everyone soaked up their charm with the adoration they commanded. I did, however, notice that their demeanor changed when someone had something positive to say about me, or showed me any interest. My partner would ensure that the conversation and attention were redirected back to them. I was made to believe that I was not worthy of praise, and that people were only feeling sorry for me. I adapted to my way of life because I believed that this was how relationships were meant to be. I lived in hope that they would be happy with everything I was doing for them. I held onto the glimmer of hope that I would be rewarded with some of the love and affection I craved. My flame of hope slowly diminished when I realized that I would never measure up to my partner's expectations.

Where was I going wrong? Why won't my partner shower me with affection? I needed to understand what the problem was so that I could rectify it. I turned to my computer and started typing in phrases that referred me to various articles, blog posts, or forums. I read through everything so that I could understand. I was so fixated on working on becoming a better person for my partner, that I discovered that I got lost in transit. I didn't realize that my partner had been filling my mind with doubts and negative thoughts during our relationship. My partner had manipulated my mind into believing that I was at fault. Everything that happened during our relationship was crafted on their terms. They chose when I would receive a hint of the affection I craved, how I would get it, and why I deserved it. I don't believe I ever had an opportunity to enjoy those hints because, in the blink of an eye, my partner removed all traces of evidence. The information I had found was starting to add up. I was in a relationship with a *narcissist*.

## Understanding Narcissism

I needed to look at the definition of what a narcissist was before I could continue to put the pieces of the puzzle together. I consulted the Merriam-Webster online dictionary for an official definition. The first entry in the dictionary defines narcissists or narcissistic behaviors as individuals who are self-centered and obsessed with their physical appearance, as well as portraying themselves as important figures in their family, work, or social settings (Merriam-Webster, n.d.). The first thought that entered my mind, when I read the definition, was that narcissists resemble peacocks. They command the attention of onlookers by fluffing their plumes for all to admire. They create a theatrical performance as they strut their beautiful colors, patterns, and voices as they parade themselves around.

I continued with my research and the words "narcissistic personality disorder (NPD)" grabbed hold of my attention. I stared at the name and I felt a wave of relief wash over me. I had, with the help of online medical professionals, diagnosed my partner. I continued reading the symptoms and causes of this disorder. I read through everything, and held my breath in anticipation as I looked for the treatment section. My heart dropped to my toes when I discovered that there was no medication or actual treatment that I could administer to help my partner. Everything that was suggested would have to be initiated by them. I knew that my partner would never agree to any type of treatment because they didn't believe that they were at fault. They lived in a world where only they existed.

I want to share everything I have learned during this difficult process. The information I have gathered comes from multiple sources. It was an eye-opening experience for me. I had never realized how many people were in the same position as I was. The personal experiences that were being shared with me had my skin crawling and the hairs on the back of my neck standing to attention. My initial reaction was that of shock, and then I felt sorry for what people were, and are still, going through. People are filled with fear and shame—fear to leave the situation, and shame because of all they have had to endure. Help is on the way; just hang in there until the end of this book.

## *Narcissistic Personality Disorder: Signs, Symptoms, and Causes*

Everything that I have presented to you about narcissism and narcissists has been neatly put together under the formal name of narcissistic personality disorder. This disorder is one of the many mental conditions that people could be diagnosed with. There is no selection order when it comes to who are narcissists, and NPD does not discriminate against who will be picked to join the following. Narcissists are clever people who know how to get what they want, but it is also believed that they are very insecure. They don't want their victims to see the cracks in their tough exteriors; but, beneath that layer of confidence, they are afraid of losing all credibility once they are exposed. Let's take a closer look at some of the signs and symptoms of people who have been diagnosed with NPD.

## *Signs and Symptoms*

It is important to identify the signs and symptoms of NPD before we can look at the causes. We need to find a common thread between the way people act and what is influencing them. Remember that the signs and symptoms I will be sharing may vary from person to person, and situation to situation. The following list is a guide to help you identify possible narcissistic behaviors among your partner, family members, or friends. Remember that only medical professionals can confirm a diagnosis, so I wouldn't want you to go around accusing people of having NDP when they haven't been properly diagnosed.

What we have learned thus far about narcissists is that they want to be in the spotlight at all times. They demand and command attention. They want the praise that they believe they deserve and have earned. These are just two drops in a large bucket full of examples.

They believe that their accomplishments in the workplace or life are more important than someone who has worked their tails off to reach the top.

Every word out of their mouths is about "me, myself, and I."

They have no problem chiming in when they feel that they are being edged out of someone's shining moment.

They embellish their achievements to make themselves seem superior.

They speak down to people who don't fall into their category of superiority.

They will strive to be, and have, the best.

Their lives are about having trophies that they can show off—the trophy partner, the trophy vehicle, or the trophy job.

Narcissists are quick to help others, only to throw it in their faces when they feel as though they are not getting the attention they demand.

Narcissists will not hesitate to make others feel as though they owe the person a debt of gratitude for helping them.

Narcissists are jealous when others are being praised for their humility.

People with narcissistic tendencies are arrogant and believe that other people should be grateful to walk in their shadows.

Narcissists are entitled and demand that others do the work for them so that they don't have to get their hands dirty.

As I have previously mentioned, this list gives you a rough idea of how narcissists operate. Some may be more subtle than others, but their true colors will shine through when they have bagged their victims. Narcissists hide behind many masks that will change according to what they want to portray to you and others.

## *Causes*

I have seen many people wonder about the most common causes that lead to being diagnosed with NPD. I find it heartwarming that people want to take whatever precautions are necessary to protect those they care about. If only it were as easy as ensuring that they dress warmly so that they won't catch a chill, or preventing them from eating tainted food to avoid food poisoning. I have learned that people are not born with NPD, it is something that they "grow" into. The causes of NPD are not as easily determined as a flu virus, cancer, or any other diseases or disorders. It is possible that the causes of NPD may include various factors which include:

trauma stemming from physical, emotional, verbal, and sexual abuse from their childhood

the type of relationship experienced with parents, siblings, family, or friends when they were growing up

a family history of NPD

an altered state of mind between their brain, behavior, and the way they think

parents neglecting them or overprotecting them during their formative years

parents raising the bar of expectation unnecessarily high, and enforcing strict rules to achieve desired results for the children

## *Narcissistic Personality Disorder: Traits and Characteristics*

Narcissists have no shame in sharing the best of themselves. They believe that they are the best of the best, and no one can measure up to them. They have set their bars so high that I doubt that they can even reach the top spot. I like to believe that all narcissists belong to an exclusive club where they feed off each other to become the greatest in their field of narcissistic personality disorder torture. I have previously touched on some of the traits and characteristics of narcissists. I think that it is important to touch on these again, so that the victims can see them. The more they see what is being said, the more likely they are to recognize their abuser. I know that victims are reading what is being said, but they have an excuse for everything that is pointing at the abuser. I get it. I was there, too. My shoulders were sagging under the weight of the blame that I had loaded onto myself. The blinders came off, and I could see clearly.

I have consulted various online publications and articles that were written by medical professionals, medical journalists, or everyday people who have been where you are. I took all the information I have accumulated and put together a compilation of traits and characteristics, for ease of reference.

### *Devoid of Empathy*

Narcissists don't know how to feel sorry for someone else if it doesn't benefit them. They don't care about how someone else is feeling or what they may be going through. The narcissist will become annoyed with people who express their feelings of sadness, grief, joy, or happiness. They will say things that are hurtful or malicious to the person who needs comfort during their time of sadness. Narcissists will change the direction of the conversation so that the attention is returned to them. In short, they don't care about anyone else, regardless of whether it is family, friends, or their partners.

## *Superiority*

One of the most stand-out traits of a narcissist is the flair of grandiosity that they portray. This is, most probably, one of the first signs that point you in the direction of the narcissist highway. They will start embellishing their accomplishments very subtly. The masks start falling away, the further along the relationship progresses. Their superiority sets them on a pedestal three feet above everyone else. They will not hesitate to fabricate stories that will elevate them even higher because, in their world, no one else can do what they can do. Everything is about their brilliance, their success, their place in the company or the community, or the way they express their love and adoration for others in front of an audience.

## *Manipulative and Controlling*

Narcissists have many underlying issues when it comes to attachment and dependency issues. I have previously mentioned that narcissists are master manipulators who will stop at nothing to get what they want. They have to control everything, and they will do whatever it takes to reach their goal. Narcissists thrive off the feedback they receive from people who are blinded by their manipulation tactics. There is no hesitation from their side when they are dazzling onlookers with what might look like a perfect, loving relationship. They have to create the smokescreen that they are the perfect, loving, and caring partner. The smokescreen they hide behind is nothing more than an illusion of what happens when their audience leaves. Narcissists are crafty, and will have you believing and doing everything that they want from you without breaking a sweat.

### *Self-Centered*

This is one of the traits that have been mentioned previously, and that emit silent warning alarms. Narcissists love attention. They thrive off the attention. They will find all the spotlights and have them redirected to where they are. Narcissists are self-appointed spokespeople for all conversations. They can hijack the conversations and bring in a bigger crowd because they ooze confidence. Narcissists don't handle rejection very well. They will change their performance when they start noticing that their audience is no longer interested. They become panicked and feel defeated when their spotlight begins dimming. Narcissists will view this as a failure, and most likely take it out on those who are closest to them.

## *Narcissistic Personality Disorder: The Side Effects*

I have shown you signs, symptoms, causes, traits, and characteristics that may help you identify a narcissist in your midst. I know that a lot of what I have shared may identify with loved ones, family, or friends. I don't doubt that everyone has some narcissistic traits flowing through their veins. Everyone wants to be acknowledged for their accomplishments, they want the praise they deserve for a task well-done, or they need the caring and loving support of loved ones during difficult times. The biggest difference, I believe, is that *normal* people are happy with someone saying "good job;" "keep it up;" or "I'm sorry you're not well."

Someone with NPD will crash and burn if they don't get what they demand. They will become a hazard to themselves or those around them. Narcissists spend so much of their time and energy reaching the summit of the mountain. It is a disappointment and a sign of weakness when they can no longer progress. There is only one thing to do when you reach the top, and that is to start the descent. Narcissists see this as a failure, and when someone feels as if they have failed at something, they take it personally. Unfortunately, they don't know how to deal with their failures, and this makes them susceptible to a host of mental and physical health conditions which may include:

depression

anxiety

isolation from society

relationship problems

heart conditions

turning to habit-forming substances such as drinking alcohol, smoking, or misusing prescription or illegal drugs

becoming abusive or aggressive

thinking about suicide or self-harming

I think I can speak up for people who have been in narcissistic relationships. I know that we don't wish harm on anyone, regardless of what they may have done to us. I would like to see my partner getting the treatment and healing that is needed, so that they won't put future partners through the agony that I endured. I can't seem to move past the list of possible complications that my partner may experience. Please don't misunderstand—I am happy that I broke free from the reign of terror when I walked away. I left with some dignity still intact, and the healing from that relationship is still a work in progress. I just don't believe that anyone would wish heart conditions or suicide on their worst enemies, regardless of what they went through. I certainly wouldn't wish ill on anyone because I know that karma strikes when we least expect it.

# Chapter 2:

# The Myths of Narcissistic Abuse

You learned the definition of narcissism in the previous chapter. You were also introduced to the signs, symptoms, causes, and side effects. I know that many people may not agree with the label of narcissism, narcissist, or any other of the terminology that points in that direction. How would you feel if I told you that narcissism was not thought up by someone overnight? Medical professionals may be foaming at the mouth because they want to believe that they coined the term. The first person to identify that narcissism was a mental disorder was a British physician by the name of Havelock Ellis. The discovery occurred in 1898. It is believed that a mythological figure, Narcissus, inspired the name of the disorder because he was in love with his reflection.

Researchers from the American Psychological Association (APA) conducted studies to find out if narcissism and aggression were linked. A total of 123,043 participants, across 437 studies, were interviewed and evaluated. The outcome of the research concluded that aggression and violence were related to narcissism (Kjærvik & Bushman, 2021).

A narcissistic personality disorder is less common than one might like to believe. That is according to an article written for The Recovery Village, in Florida. The staff writers, members of various medical backgrounds such as psychiatry, psychology, and registered nurses, have shared statistics relating to the prevalence of NPD in the United States of America. It is believed that approximately 0.5% of Americans, across the 50 states, have been diagnosed with NPD. That means that one in every 200 people in the United States has NPD. It is further believed that approximately 75% of the people who have been diagnosed with NPD are men (The Recovery Village, 2021).

The United States of America is not the only country with people who suffer from personality disorders. Scientists collected data from 21 countries spanning six continents. A total of 46 different studies were conducted which showed that approximately 7.8% of the global population has a personality disorder. This percentage ranges across various spectrums which include high- and low-income individuals, graduates, and other types of occupations (Winsper et al., 2019).

# Debunking Misconceptions Regarding Narcissistic Abuse

The dictionary tells us that myths are popular stories or assumptions we learned from our parents, grandparents, educators, or people we trusted (Merriam-Webster, 2018). We didn't have any reason to doubt what they said—that is until we reached the age where we could do our own research. I don't believe that they intended to deceive us, and it could be that they were sharing what they had learned when they were younger.

Myths become dangerous when someone's health and well-being are at stake. I think it is safe to assume that we saw many medical students graduate from the esteemed *Google Sofa Medical University* in 2020 and 2021. Everyone became an expert in some medical field whether it was an epidemiologist, a general practitioner, or a psychologist. Everyone had an opinion. I get it—we had more time on our hands than we knew what to do with. Oh, we could bake banana and sourdough bread every day, but that trend died out around the three-month mark of quarantine. It was during this time that we learned that conspiracy theorists were rife among the social media communities. I remember reading advice, about drinking bleach or hand sanitizer to kill a virus, that was causing panic across the globe.

I have found that people see or hear something, and they form their own conclusions. They will read the first and last paragraph of an article, and claim that they know everything. One thing I want to highlight here, which is something everyone needs to understand and remember, is that you should not be playing Russian roulette with your mental, emotional, or physical health. This is where myths become dangerous because people believe what the grocers, hairdressers, or trucker boyfriend tells. Ever heard of the broken telephone game? Important information gets lost, and you are left with a half-baked myth that could be potentially life-threatening.

Narcissism is not exempt from the myths train. I know that you are full of doubts because you may still be holding onto some hope that you have an overactive imagination. Someone may have sent you a link to a blog that tells you that whatever you are experiencing is normal. I've told you before, and I'm going to tell you again, but I have a moral obligation to be truthful. I was where you are. I, too, didn't want to believe the evidence that I was presented with. I was in denial, but my eyes opened when I started comparing the myths to what was happening daily. That is why I am here, writing this book, to help you compare some of the myths that you don't want to believe. Reach out to a medical professional if you need more confirmation.

## *Debunked Myth #1: It's Not Abuse if You Don't Have Scars*

Abuse—whether physical, sexual, verbal, or emotional—is abuse. Not all forms of abuse leave visible lesions, bruises, or scars. Narcissists, as we have previously discussed, are clever and will find ways to hurt their partners, family members, or friends without leaving physical scars. I remember a rhyme from my childhood years, something that I never paid attention to until I found myself in a relationship with a narcissist: *Sticks and stones may break my bones, but words will never hurt me.* Whoever came up with this proverb should face public flogging. The implication is that bones, lesions, and bruises will heal and fade away—out of sight and out of mind. The part that upset me, when I realized what it meant, was that words wouldn't hurt. I have met many people during the research of this book. Everyone, both men and women, have told me that they are haunted by hurtful words when they close their eyes, or taunted when they are working. Always remember that just because you can't see any physical signs of abuse, does not mean that someone isn't abused.

## *Debunked Myth #2: Don't Be Fooled by Picture Perfect Facades*

I am reminded of the photos of happy, smiling families you see in photo frames at the store, or even images used to advertise products. Everyone looks so happy, the adults are gazing into each other's eyes with love and adoration, and the children are happy to be part of their loving family. Advertising and marketing agencies don't seem to understand that they are selling a false narrative to others who see what is being advertised. It may just be that someone is looking at the product that is being advertised, and they believe that by purchasing the product, they too will be happy. It is hard to believe that those beautiful smiles of love, adoration, and joy could possibly be hiding some heartbreaking secrets of domestic violence, sexual abuse, or emotional abuse.

Narcissists are clever. They can make everyone believe that they are part of a loving family unit. If someone were to comment about a partner looking a little sad, down, or withdrawn, they would not hesitate to pack on the charm to change their view. Don't always assume that all is good and well when you have spotted some red flags. Don't dismiss your instincts because someone dresses well, earns a decent salary, or provides their families with the best of everything. There is no one-size-fits-all when it comes to narcissistic abusers.

## *Debunked Myth #3: All Mental Illnesses Are Diagnosed and Treated*

The truth is that not all mental illnesses are diagnosed or treated. It is believed that approximately 50% of the U.S. population is not receiving the treatment that they need (Mental Illness Policy Org, 2016).

Another publication puts the ratio into perspective after a year-long study between 2015 and 2o16, whereby approximately 43% of Americans received treatment for their mental illnesses. The study claims that men are at a disadvantage because most will not receive the treatment. Furthermore, the study reveals approximately two-thirds of the population are either not diagnosed with a mental illness, or their diagnosis will go untreated (Ellis, 2019).

People are reluctant to consult medical professionals because they don't want to hear the truth, especially when it concerns their mental or physical health. You have gained a fair amount of knowledge about narcissists and their personalities since we embarked on this journey. One of the key takeaways that you have tucked into your knowledge piggy bank is that narcissists don't believe there is anything wrong with them. I like to think that subconsciously they know what they are doing, but they will not show their vulnerability by acknowledging their mental status in front of anyone. No amount of begging or pleading will see them admit that they have a problem and, instead, they will deflect all commentary onto their partners, family, or friends. They will not take responsibility for their actions, nor will they participate in any form of rehabilitation. I will end this section with a little quote that I believe sums up everything that has been mentioned: *A narcissistic personality disorder is the only mental condition where the patient is left alone but everyone else needs treatment.* —Anonymous

## *Debunked Myth #4: It Won't Happen Again*

If I had a dollar for each time someone defended an abusive partner, I would be flying to my local Target in a space capsule. Narcissistic abusers have short fuses that will ignite faster than a pin being removed from a grenade.

*It won't happen again.*

*My partner couldn't help it when they lost control.*

*My partner is under a lot of stress.*

*It was my fault they lost control.*

The victims in these situations are afraid of what their narcissistic abusive partners, family, or friends will do. I am again reminded that my abusive partner bedazzled everyone they encountered to show me how powerful they were. They knew that the more they bedazzled my family and friends, the more I would lose all credibility when I told everyone what my partner was doing to me.

Once is all it takes for a habit to start forming. Your narcissistic representative knows what they are doing the moment they do it. Some may even follow up with an "I'm sorry;" "please forgive me;" or "it won't happen again." Every narcissist that roams freely across the ground we walk on is equipped with a switch that they know how to control. Don't ever believe that they won't use it once, twice, or multiple times to get the results that they want. Everyone has a choice in life, and narcissists are not exempt. They choose what they want to do, when they will do it, and who they will do it to. They choose to charm the socks of their colleagues, or physically, mentally, or vocally abuse the people in their close circle. Remember that all it takes is once, which is already one too many.

## *Debunked Myth #5: Passes for Difficult Childhoods*

This is a myth that holds no weight, whatsoever. I have met with, and spoken to, many people who have come from various backgrounds of childhood trauma. I have seen how they interact with their children, their loved ones, and others around them. It is part of your caring and loving nature to make excuses for your narcissistic partner's actions. How many times will you make those excuses before someone, or even yourself, is hurt to the point where you lose your voice. Remember, once is all that is needed for a narcissistic abuser to form an ongoing habit. We need to break the silence surrounding the excuses we fabricate to defend abusers.

I think that it is safe to say that no one wants to see you in the hospital, cowering in a corner, or on the ground because you gave your abuser multiple passes for their childhood experiences. You can break that cycle by standing up and saying, "no more." You have choices, and one of the most important choices you have is to stop protecting and defending them.

## *Debunked Myth #6: Forgiveness for Being Nice*

How many times have you forgiven your narcissistic abuser for apologizing for their actions? Would your answer be once, twice, or too many to count on two hands? I like to believe that everyone is nice, and that includes narcissists. I also believe that everyone has a bad day when they are grumpy, say things that might not be nice, or their actions speak louder than words. Everyone—including you, me, and the entire human race—is allowed off days. Most people have a conscience where they know that they have acted inappropriately; they apologize for their actions.

Narcissists are also nice people. They are especially nice when their egos are not being threatened by someone trying to steal their spotlight. One may even say that narcissists are fun-loving partners, parents, colleagues, or family members who enjoy spending time with the people who care about them. It is heartwarming to observe them when their guards are down. It is enough to forgive them for everything they have ever said or done to earn them the label of a narcissistic abuser. It can all change, in the blink of an eye. They are transformed back to the narcissistic abuser the moment they feel threatened or their attention spotlight begins to dim.

How many times will you continue to forgive your narcissistic partner for being nice one moment and an emotional, physical, or verbal abuser the next? This is a question we should ask all victims. Remember, once is all it takes to change the course of someone's life forever.

## *Debunked Myth #7: Other People Experience Abuse, Not Me*

Join me in setting up this myth on the football field, taking a couple of steps back, and kicking it out of the stadium. I have said it before, and I will continue repeating it until you realize that you need to see the abuse for what it is. Our narcissistic representatives have done a pretty good conditioning job on us to make us believe that we weren't, aren't, and will never be victims of abuse. Yes, they will tell you, me, and anyone who will listen to them that you are fabricating stories and events to suit your narratives. It is time to break the never-ending cycle of believing that it can't happen to us, when in fact it can happen to us. It happens to us multiple times a day.

Narcissistic abusers know what they are doing. They will tell you whatever they deem necessary to have you doubting yourself. The abuse—whether verbally, physically, mentally, or sexually—will gradually increase over time. Some people don't even notice that they are being conditioned, which is why victims will believe whatever they are told. Others may see the writing on the wall and reach out with advice, but the victim will turn off their defensive mode and continue to live in denial. This can, and most probably will, continue for many years. Victims may remember someone issuing them a warning or an observation. Victims may then sit at attention and take mental notes to keep tabs on the pattern. Abusive relationships are more common than what we would like to believe. Acknowledging that you are in trouble is not a sign of weakness or giving in to your abuser; it is a sign that you are stronger than what you believe.

## *Debunked Myth #8: Confidence Is an Olympic Sport*

This is another one of those myths that you would want to pinch up between your two fingers, walk over to the trash compactor, hit the button, and listen to it crunch as it gets crushed. We know that narcissists want to believe everything they tell themselves. They believe that they ooze confidence. They believe that they are untouchable and that they are unstoppable. Narcissists may believe that they are the bees' knees, but they are no more confident than the next person. Everyone, regardless of who they are and what they do, has doubt and fear in their genetic DNA. Some may hide it better than others, but to say that someone is confident 24–7 is wholly inaccurate.

Narcissists are afraid of being caught, hence their tough nut exterior and need to impress others. They know that if they are busted, they will lose their place in the spotlight and risk looking like the weakling that they most likely are. Narcissists don't want people to see their flaws, because that will fill them with negative thoughts and feelings of being embarrassed. After all, even though narcissists are manipulative and make others feel insignificant, they are still people who have feelings. I don't believe for one moment that anyone wishes harm upon anyone else, whether they are narcissists or not. Remember that, when I started this book, I told you there would be no bullying, judgment, or condemnation. We are here to find out why our narcissistic abusers are doing what they're doing, and help everyone find a solution that will be beneficial to all parties involved.

# Chapter 3:
# Types of Narcissistic Abuse

You may have noticed that I like to insert definitions or meanings of the words, or the topic, that will be focused on in a chapter, or section of a chapter. I do this so that you can be prepared for the subject. I also know that many people will use all these words, but when asked to give a definition, most people will struggle to explain it. There is no shame on anyone if that happens, because we are human. Our minds are like sponges that tend to soak up everything we hear without properly understanding the context in which it is used. The focus word for this chapter is *abuse*. This is a word that is used, both in and out of context, without much thought. I have heard many people use the word in a joking manner. I have also heard it being used by people who feel as if they need to be heard.

Let's consult my trusted Merriam-Webster online dictionary for guidance. Abuse can be used as a noun or a verb. Abuse is defined as the improper or excessive use of prescription or illegal medications or drugs; the use of vindictive, belittling, or choice words or language intended to break someone's spirit, or physically harming people with malicious intentions. The next time you hear someone refer to being abused in a joking manner, you may want to set the record straight because the topic of abuse is serious, with negative and harmful intentions (Merriam-Webster, 2019a).

This chapter is going to be a tough one. You may find that wounds could be opened, skeletons may jump out of the closet, or fear will threaten to strangle you. I want you to know that this chapter is not out to harm you. I want it to help you identify triggers that you may not want to acknowledge. I know the pain you must be experiencing. It is a pain that will be with you for months, or even years. My partner was emotionally, verbally, and physically abusive. I discovered how exhausting it was to be emotionally abused by their repetitive lying. The trust I had in my partner eroded. I no longer trusted nor respected them because of the constant lying, the blame for reasons unknown, and the obvious pleasure of watching me grovel for forgiveness.

Always remember that the punches that result in split lips and bruises, or the broken bones from being thrown against walls, will heal and fade. Unfortunately, the same cannot be said for the tongue and mind, which do more damage than anyone will ever know. Narcissistic abusers don't have filters in front of their mouths. They will attempt to break their victims in any way that they can. My narcissistic partner thought that they had worn me down and weakened my defenses so that I would believe everything they said about me. I showed them who they were dealing with because I realized, and finally understood, that I was a strong person who didn't have to cower in the shadows.

## Emotional Abuse

Narcissists know how to manipulate their partners' emotions. They will go for the jugular because they know their weaknesses. Narcissistic abusers, whether men or women, will gather as much of their partner's weaknesses as they can find. Everything will be stored in secured archives in their minds until they are ready to strike. We know that narcissists are crafty, and they will not hesitate to play whatever cards they have to break their partners. You may be wondering what constitutes emotional abuse. I'm so happy that you're wondering, because I'm more than happy to share everything that I have learned through personal experiences, as well as everything I've read. Take a deep breath and remember that you are in a safe space where the words that you'll be reading cannot hurt you.

A relationship is when two or more people are connected because they share a special bond or a kinship—normally childhood friends, family, or colleagues. Another type of relationship is when two people are connected because they are romantically involved or married. I'm not going to tell you that family, friends, or colleagues won't abuse you in some way, shape, or form because that would be a lie.

Narcissism is rife in families, in friendships, at work, and especially in romantic situations.

Emotional abuse occurs when one person, the narcissist in the relationship, steps up onto their invisible pedestal and assumes the role of the dictator. They take their role very seriously and will not hesitate to fill their victims with fear, lather on the criticism, or embarrass and shame them for not meeting the standards prescribed by the abuser. Narcissistic abusers will play the cards they have accumulated during their ammunition-hunting expedition. They will start with small pellets and work themselves up to cannon balls until they have broken their partners' spirits. The victims will begin to believe everything that their abusers tell them. Narcissistic abusers will have built a remote-controlled person who has been created in their image and programmed to perform as they had designed.

I would like to say that you shouldn't allow your abuser to gain entry to your mind, but I know that is not always possible. Instead, I am going to give you a list of possible emotional abusive tactics that your abuser will use to build up their arsenal. Always be vigilant because you won't know when the first attack will occur.

They will ignore you or give you the silent treatment, for no apparent reason.

They will call you names based on your weaknesses.

They will shame you for eating a piece of candy, or because you dropped your keys—anything is fair game to abusers.

They will punish you for ignoring affection such as a hug, a kiss, or a smile.

They will accuse you of being deceitful, cheating, or spending more money than you have claimed.

They will humiliate you in front of family, friends, or strangers at the store.

They will make you feel guilty because they couldn't be part of whatever you did.

Narcissistic abusers will always make you feel insignificant when you tell them that they are not treating you the way you deserve to be treated—with love and respect.

## *Under the Microscope: Identifying Emotional Abuse*

I read an article in which the author noted that not all people who are diagnosed with NPD are abusers. I had to stop and think about that for a moment. The article continues to say that people with NPD may try to abuse people, but may not succeed. You don't need to be diagnosed or have any types of labels to be an abuser. I know of people who have been at the receiving end of telemarketing cold callers who will use their charm to manipulate people by honing in on their weaknesses. Abuse is all around us, so always be aware of the subtle signs that will creep into a conversation or situation. I think we may have just given our narcissistic abusers a very slight reprieve. However, we are not going to let them off the hook, because we know what they are capable of doing.

### *Definitive Signs of Emotional Abuse*

What are some of the more definitive signs of emotional abuse in a relationship? We may have covered some of the signs in previous chapters; but again, the more you read about them, the more likely you are to identify them sooner. I believe that it is important to keep sharing the definitive signs of all forms of abuse, especially emotional abuse that occurs in relationships. Always remember that the warning signs are all around us. Some of the most common characteristics of NPD emotional abuse include:

their dominating presence as they enter any room or area, because they believe that they are more important than anyone else

the need to inflate their egos by ensuring that the focus is on them, and that they are admired by everyone within their line of vision

the belief that they are owed attention, respect, admiration, and everything that will ensure that they are on a diamond-encrusted platinum pedestal

I recently watched a YouTube video where someone made a very narcissistic comment. The comment relates to one of the characteristics which narcissists will use, which is the lack of empathy. The video showed a content creator talking about the death of a family member. Another content creator, who had beef with almost all the creators that produce similar types of content, sent a message offering their "condolences." The message was along the lines of "that's too bad" when they were told that a child—let that sink in—a child had died, and the response was "that's too bad."

### *Subtle Signs of Emotional Abuse*

Narcissist abusers have more tricks up their sleeves than one may think. We have covered many of their traits since the start of this journey. We're not here to make excuses for our narcissistic partners. They will not take responsibility for their actions, but that doesn't mean that you, me, or others need to be held accountable. Their narcissistic tendencies will have you assuming the blame for what they have or are doing. I want you to know that it is not your fault. You are not crazy. You are not losing your mind. Let's take a look at some more signs that your narcissistic partner may pack on your shoulders.

They will fill your mind with doubt when you know you did something, and they are telling you that you are making up stories.

They'll make you believe that you are not invested in the relationship, and blame you for lack of communication, affection, and adoration.

They will send mixed signals in an attempt to confuse, such as being nasty, cruel, and hurtful, and then shower you with gifts.

The power struggle may be one of the worst because they will have you believe that you are in control, but the reality is that they are controlling the situation.

They will criticize everything you do: from the way you dress for work, cook dinner, or interact with your children.

They will accuse you of something, backtrack, and deny that they were doing anything of the sort.

## *Under the Microscope: The Side Effects of Emotional Abuse*

I have met many people from all walks of life who have shared their experiences of narcissistic abuse with me. Some were in their relationships for more than 30 years before they escaped their hell. Others have said that they never experienced any type of trauma from being in a narcissistic relationship. Some shared their side effects in as much detail as they could because they want everyone to be aware of what they may or may not be experiencing. I do believe that everyone who has been in any type of abusive relationship has some residual post-traumatic stress when they walk away. Can I share a little secret with you? There is no shame in admitting that you are suffering from any form of post-abusive relationship side effects. There is also no shame in seeking professional advice to help you deal with these deeply in-grained side effects. I would like you to throw the doors wide open and manifest that you are not going to be held captive by your abusers' slanderous treatment of you. Please keep in mind that this is not a competition to see who has the most side effects or who has lingering effects. There will be no prizes, awards, or any type of shout-out, other than to tell you that you are brave, strong, and amazing for finding and setting yourself free.

Let's take a look at some of the short-term and long-term side effects that you may be experiencing. The following list could potentially make your day-to-day life difficult and unmanageable. Don't ever be afraid to reach out for help. Someone is always willing and able to help you.

### *Short-Term Side Effects*

feeling dazed and confused—not knowing what you should be doing

feeling as if your heart is going to break through your chest cavity because of anxiety

being embarrassed or filled with shame because your relationship fell apart being overwhelmed with emotions and uncontrollable crying, which ties in with anxiety

feeling as if you need to justify everything you say or do

feeling as if you don't have control over the way you think about doing or saying something, or the way you act when faced with a suggestion

***Long-Term Side Effects***

depression

anxiety disorder

using and abusing habit-forming substances such as illegal or prescription drugs and medication, smoking, or alcohol

struggling with chronic pain that will often have you feeling debilitated

# Verbal Abuse

I previously mentioned the "sticks and stones" proverb that we learned as children. I do believe that I made my feelings about that proverb very clear. I would say that "words will never hurt" is a very narcissistic expression because words hurt more than physical pain. A narcissistic partner, colleague, friend, or family member will use their words to break your spirit. They will repeat their hurtful chants, until you believe that what is being said is true. You will start doubting yourself. You will lose faith in your ability to perform tasks. You will feel defeated. It sounds a lot like emotional abuse—right? That is because the two are closely related, and they are training your mind by manipulating and dominating the way you think. In short, your narcissistic counterparts want to control you. They won't want to relinquish the power they have over you, and they will stop at nothing to keep you hostage in their warped worlds.

I would like to add that verbal abuse is not to be confused with an argument between people. You shouldn't automatically assume someone is being verbally abused when you hear raised voices. We know that narcissists are cunning, and they will want to be careful during their attacks. They are a lot more subtle about planning and executing their plans of action. This is one of the reasons why many people have said that they were never verbally abused by their narcissistic partners, friends, family, or colleagues. Almost everyone I know associates verbal abuse with screaming matches between two people which normally involve glasses, plates, or something being thrown around. I'm not going to say that this is not true, but I also want you to be aware that verbal abuse involves a whole lot more than screaming, shouting, and slinging around words that should be buried in the garden.

I gave you a list of different types of emotional abuse that your narcissist may use to break you. I thought it would be fitting to share a similar list that highlights some of the different types of verbal abusive tactics. The list may resemble many of the points previously listed, but as I've said before, I'd rather you see it mentioned more than a couple of times than caught unawares. Something will resonate with what you, or someone close to you, may be experiencing, and then you'll erect your defenses until you can break away.

I like to call this "passing the buck" because the narcissistic abusers will blame their victims for the verbal abuse they're receiving, and insinuate that they brought this upon themselves.

Narcissistic abusers will defame and insult their victims by calling them abusive names in an attempt to embarrass, belittle, hurt, or break them down.

Narcissists enjoy scaring their victims with thinly veiled threats, and they are rather crafty with this little game because they will make you believe that you were imagining what they were saying.

Another thing about threats is that abusers will use this tactic to scare their victims into believing that people outside of their world are seeing the victim as the problem in the situation—manipulation at its worst.

Criticism is a lovely little game that narcissists like to play with their victims, where they will pass nasty and hard-to-hear remarks to embarrass the victims.

Criticism in a normal relationship or setting is used to help build people up, but this does not ring true for narcissistic relationships where the abusers are purposely and deliberately using their words and actions to break their victims.

I promised to protect you from being judged or bullied because no one has the right to look down on anyone or pass any form of judgment based on who they are, what their circumstances are, where they are from, or why they are in the position they are in.

Narcissists thrive on anxiety and discomfort by judging their partners for their past wrongdoings, which may include sexual immorality, committing unintentional fraud, or wishing ill harm to family members.

## *Under the Microscope: Identifying Verbal Abuse*

You may still be in denial and say that your narcissistic partner is not verbally abusing you. Your reasoning may be that they are protecting you from others who have ill intentions towards you. The list of different types of narcissistic verbal abuse doesn't apply to you because your partner would never hurt you. It is time to get yourself a good eye-washing solution and do a thorough clean. Next, you will want to take a notebook and pen, and hide in the closet while you write down a list of "lovable" words and actions your partner, friend, colleague, or family member has said to you in the last six months. Be honest with yourself because, remember, you haven't been verbally or emotionally abused—ever.

I am not here labeling you as a liar or doubting you, because that's not why I'm here. I want you to see what is going on around you. Remember that I have been where you are and I, too, lived in denial alley for many years. You may not even realize that your narcissistic partner is, or has been, verbally abusing you. I do know that, when you start reading through the tactics, signs, and side effects, something is going to resonate with you. I can also tell you that you are going to experience a rush of cold air when the realization sinks in. I want to prepare you for the realization and help you realize that you are not alone.

### *Signs of Narcissistic Verbal Abuse*

I know that your mind is working overtime to sort through and digest everything you have learned during this section. You may still be denying that you are or were verbally abused. You might not even be certain that your partner is a narcissist. I can't force you to believe anything you are not willing to accept. That is why I repeat a lot of the traits, signs, and whatever else is important. The information I am sharing is not pulled out of thin air. Everything that you are reading is based on personal experiences and information from licensed therapists. I'm sharing this with you and hope you know that I am not coming after you or trying to convince you that you are in a narcissistic relationship.

The traits you have learned about may mirror the signs but, as I have mentioned a couple of times, you have to remember the "sticks and stones" proverb. Words and actions hurt worse than anything you may have ever experienced. Once your brain processes the hurtful words, those words will stick like glue and will continue packing on until you do something to break the cycle—that is a subject for another discussion. The bottom line is that you need to know, see, and understand what you are experiencing through the words of a stranger. Don't worry—I will have the virtual Kleenex ready to dab the tears, and I'll be right here should you need a virtual hug.

I have mentioned some of the traits which included name-calling, criticizing, judging, bullying, threatening, and thriving on their victim's anxiety and insecurities. Many of the signs of narcissistic verbally abused victims include the traits, as well. Narcissists will play their hands at any opportunity they can to show their victims who is in charge and who has the power. I have compiled a list of signs that were shared by victims who have been where you are. They didn't believe that they were being verbally abused, either, until they looked at their lives through a microscope. What do you think they realized? Let's take a look to see if anything resonates with you.

Your partner shows you off as some treasured possession when attending work, social, or family events.

They will ensure that you are close to them at all times, most likely to make sure that you don't steal their thunder or say something negatively.

Whispering in your ear may not be the romantic notion others may believe; instead, it is a threat and warning to keep you in line.

Your narcissistic partner will fill your head with doubts regarding decisions being made, and you will relinquish control to them or follow what they want—good or bad.

You become skittish, and the doubt you feel is amplified by anxiety and fear.

Going on vacation, or attending family events for the holidays, once filled you with excitement; but, somewhere along the way, that happy-go-lucky feeling was snuffed out.

Your narcissistic partner may tease you about an upcoming event, and you allow yourself to become excited—until they pull back the carrot that they had dangled in front of you.

You believe everything that your partner has told you about your faults and shortcomings, and you start hearing the voices of confirmation in your mind.

The abusive words that your partner spews at you constantly taunt, condemn, and judge you because they have made you believe that you cannot measure up to their standards.

You start making up happy scenarios where you tell yourself that your partner will wake up one day, realize what they have done to you, and make amends because they have seen the error in their ways.

## *Under the Microscope: The Side Effects of Verbal Abuse*

As much as we would like to believe that everything in life is sunshine and roses, we would only be fooling ourselves. I know that we try to do the best we can with every situation we are faced with. I also know that we set ourselves very high expectations. Sometimes, we fail to get anywhere close to those expectations because of some potholes in the road. We end up standing at the fork in the road and don't know which way to go because of the situation we find ourselves in.

In the previous section, we learned about some of the side effects due to the emotional abuse our narcissistic abusers inflict on us. This section was a lot heavier because of the subtle nature of the way we are exposed to verbal abuse. We have learned that not all verbally abusive partners will raise their voices and throw things around (this does happen, too). The verbal abuse you may experience is done in such a way that you don't even realize it. If I were to be honest, I would have preferred the *screaming and throwing things around* part of the abuse. I know what it felt like to be "silently" abused. I never knew what had hit me, until I started putting the pieces of many years' worth of puzzles back together. Suddenly, everything started making sense, and that is when I knew what I had to do.

The side effects of verbal abuse, as with emotional abuse, affect our health negatively. Everything we do in life has consequences, and it doesn't matter whether we are willing participants or if it is forced on us. Let's take a look at some of the side effects of what our narcissistic partners, colleagues, friends, or family members' verbal abuse can mean for our mental, emotional, and physical health and well-being.

## *Post-Traumatic Stress Disorder (PTSD)*

Post-traumatic stress disorder (PTSD) is not only reserved for people who are (or were) in the army, have been in a devastating car accident, or may have experienced trauma such as murder, car-jacking, or sexual assault. The residual effects of being verbally and emotionally abused are prevalent in narcissistic relationships. People who are diagnosed with PTSD in verbally abusive relationships never know when their past will come back to remind them of what had happened. The victims will need therapy that will help them deal with their past, rebuild relationships, and forge new relationships going forward.

## *Being Estranged From Family and Friends*

Narcissists don't like their partners enjoying life because that would most likely take the attention away from them. They would rather spend their time telling their victims that they only want to be with them. Other victims may want to isolate themselves from their family and friends because they don't want to alert them to the abuse they are experiencing. The worst thing that an abuser will tell their victim is that nobody wants to spend time with them because they look miserable. The truth is that they don't want their victims to accidentally say something that will expose them for who and what they are. The victims are embarrassed because they believed that they were in love with their partners.

## *Low Self-Esteem*

Verbally abused victims are broken down to where they dislike themselves. They will believe all the lies their abusers tell them, and they adopt all the negative commentary. The verbal onslaught that the victims are faced with will range from being belittled and condemned to their past being thrown in front of them. They are made to feel guilty for everything that they have ever done. The person receiving the word punches is so broken that they may even turn to self-harm. They want to punish themselves for being the terrible person their partners make them believe.

### *Other Side Effects*

The side effects mentioned are just a taste of what you may be going through. Please keep remembering the "sticks and stones" rhyme, and know that you are not alone. Don't allow your abuser to tell you otherwise. Let's take a look at some other side effects that you may experience. You may be:

moody

feeling guilty

extremely lonely and craving company

depressed

suffering from anxiety

participating in the use of habit-forming substances to help you cope

## Physical Abuse

The third and final form of abuse I want to talk about is the physical side. I spoke about the emotional and verbal side of abuse that was "silent but violent" in which victims were manipulated by words and actions. Yes, I said that emotionally and verbally abused victims would experience longer-lasting side effects of narcissistic abuse. I said that because the words will always come back and stop you in your tracks when it is least expected. The hurtful words have a way of echoing through your mind to remind you where you were, currently are, and where you are heading. Months and years of therapy will help you to heal from the trauma experienced during your abusive relationship.

I experienced a sudden burst of adrenaline when I thought about what I would say about physical abuse. The sad reality is that physical abuse has the ingredients to end a life because of what someone else is doing to you. That is why I have kept this section for last. It is important for your healing that you pick up and identify all the signs and side effects of emotional and verbal abuse first. Once you have gathered and stored all the information you have learned, you can then proceed with the most violent side of narcissistic abuse. Everything you have acquired until now has been a prelude to the swan song of physical abuse.

We know that our narcissistic abusers are crafty. We know what they are capable of, and how they will twist their version of events to suit their narrative. They will even have you doubting that your version of the events is not as it seems. This is a tactic they will use when reasoning with their victims and ultimately declare themselves free of any blame. They are shameless and have no regard for the people they claim to control—I mean love. Narcissistic abusers will throw everyone, other than themselves, under the bus to divert the blame away from themselves. Their victims will carry most of the blame because that is what their abusers are telling them, by saying stuff like:

*You upset me.*

*You wouldn't do what I told you to do.*

*It is your fault.*

*I am the way I am because you choose to disrespect me.*

*You don't respect me.*

These responses are hidden between statements of love, affection, adoration, and (dare we say) half-hearted apologies. I recently spoke to someone who told me that their partner would slam them up against the wall, or start throwing punches in front of their toddler. The usual trigger for these random acts of physical abuse was related to finances. The abuser would push their partner against the wall and hold them by the throat. Then, looking at the toddler, they would threaten that they would never see their child again. The victim has been in an abusive relationship for 10 years. I know that they have been advised by family members to walk away from the relationship, but the victim is afraid that their abuser will follow through on the threats and disappear with their child. This is a scenario that may represent both men and women, but for the sake of privacy, I have omitted the genders because I have heard one too many of these types of heartbreaking stories.

## *Under the Microscope: Identifying Physical Abuse*

Identifying physical abuse may be easier than spotting verbal or emotional abuse. Wounds inflicted by your abuser can be hidden under clothing, or by applying make-up. Individuals who are physically abused may blame the sighting of visible injuries or wincing because of pain on being clumsy or an accident. Physical abuse by anyone—whether a narcissistic partner, friend, colleague, or family member—is a criminal offense and is punishable by law. The act of being physically abused fills the victim with fear because they believe that it will be a one-time event, and they take the blame for "provoking" their abuser. What constitutes physical abuse? Take a look at the following list which includes:

threatening your life with a weapon

shaking you

purposely bumping into you

throwing you against a wall

choking you

pinching you and leaving bruises

burning you with cigarettes

pulling your hair

slapping you

kicking you

punching you

sexually assaulting you

All it takes is one act of physical abuse to claim the life of a victim. Don't allow someone to rob you of your life. Easier said than done, I know, but I also know that you have the courage to do what is right for your well-being. Don't allow your abuser to form a habit of your abuse. They aren't worth it.

### *Victims of Physical Abuse*

I needed to add this little sub-section because I believe it is important to identify who is prone to physical abuse by possible narcissists. Victims of physical abuse are not always in relationships. Many victims have been placed in care facilities where their families trust that they are being cared for. We put a lot of faith in people who are trained in their fields, and rely on their expertise to do what is best for these family members. I recently heard of an incident where an elderly person was placed in a care home. This person would tell everyone that the carers were hurting them, but they were dismissed because they had been diagnosed with dementia. A family member was doing some accounting for the person and discovered that someone else was using the mobile phone.

The family member couldn't understand why the bill was sky-high, until they realized that one of the nurses had been transferring call time to their phone. The matter was directed to a senior member of the family, who in turn reported it to the police. The nurse was subsequently charged with fraud and theft, and was terminated from their job. A further investigation uncovered that the nurse had been physically and sexually molesting the vulnerable people.

People, other than partners, family, friends, or colleagues, who are affected by physical abuse include:

frail and elderly people in care homes

developmentally disabled individuals

physically disabled individuals

people with mental health issues

sexual partners

## *Under the Microscope: The Side Effects of Physical Abuse*

What are we looking for in people who have been, or are being, physically abused? Would it be someone dressed in a hoodie and sweatpants in 104°F weather? I think that would be a dead giveaway. The truth is, no one really knows what someone else is going through. I can give you some of the side effects that I have found, but no two people will experience the same level of abuse. No two people will have the same or similar scars, bruises, or hurt in their eyes. If you are reading this and you are a victim of physical abuse; please reach out to someone who will give you sound advice on what your next steps should be. Don't allow your abuser to take away more than they already have. Everyone who loves you for who and what you are wants to see the sparkle back in your eyes.

What are some of those side effects that I was talking about? Let's take a look at the list together, but please remember that what I am listing might not cover all you are experiencing. The list is merely for guidance and to give you, and others, an idea of what a victim may be experiencing:

visible bruising

excessive use of make-up

lesions

welts

broken or injured bones

cuts

open wounds

change in behavior—moody, sullen and quiet, teary, or aggressive and defensive

denied accessibility from family or friends to visit the victim

stress-related conditions such as weight loss, depression, or anxiety

insomnia

compromised immune system

dehydration

malnutrition

bedsores

an overall decline in mental and physical health

being denied food

# Chapter 4:

# All About Gaslighting

> *Gaslighting their partners into believing the abuse isn't real by denying, minimizing, or rationalizing the abuse. This includes deflecting any conversations about accountability using circular conversations and word salad in order to avoid being held accountable for their actions.* —Shahida Arabi

I believe that it is safe to assume that you are ready to proceed with the healing portion of this book. I would love to tell you that your healing begins with this chapter or the next, but then I would be lying. I don't lie because it is not going to benefit me in any way, shape, or form. However, I would like to tell you that your healing journey started the moment you purchased, or were gifted, a copy of this book. We have gone back in history, turned over stones, and crawled through tunnels. You were shown the severity of what it was like being in a relationship with a narcissist. Healing begins when you talk about your experience because you are getting it out there, instead of having it fester in your mind, body, and soul. We have to face the difficult situations we have hidden from the world because it is an uncommon belief that, when something is out of sight, it is out of mind.

This chapter is going to be the last little stepping stone before you can run, skip, and roll around in the meadow of prosperity. I want you to realize that you can break free from the trophy case your narcissistic partner, friend, colleague, or family has placed you in. I want to use this chapter to tell you about something you may have heard before. I have not mentioned it because I believed that it needed a chapter dedicated to it. I am talking about gaslighting. This is a term that has been used multiple times to describe narcissist behaviors. Gaslighting is one of the traits associated with someone who manipulates those they are holding hostage with scaremongering tactics. Narcissists are crafty critters who believe that their victims will bow to them whenever they demand. I want this chapter to be educational and help you understand a little more than what I have already discussed. You are going to:

understand what gaslighting entails

learn where it originated from

identify the signs

take a closer look at the process involved

know how it impacts your life

# Understanding Gaslighting

What do we know about gaslighting? No, I'm not talking about gas lights that you would use when you go camping. Gaslighting is something that a narcissistic person will implement as part of their manipulation of their victims. The Merriam-Webster dictionary tells us that gaslighting forms part of the emotional abuse that our narcissist abusers will do to psychologically manipulate their victims. The practice of gaslighting will occur over a period of time, and will find the victim second-guessing everything they do. The abuser will use this tactic to confuse their victims, manipulate their perceptions relating to reality, and alter their memories to fit their narratives. Narcissistic abusers take pride in their craft, and they will revel in their art as they watch their victims lose confidence in themselves, become skittish and have little to no self-confidence, and doubt their emotional and mental health. Narcissists will be waiting in the shadows as they watch their victims struggle to understand what they are going through. Remote-controlled victims will be driven into the "loving" arms of their narcissists who will whisper sweet words of nothing into their ears (Merriam-Webster, n.d.-a).

The dictionary presents us with an accurate description of all gaslighting does to the victim. I have often heard victims of abuse say that their partners didn't know what they were doing. This is what your abuser wants you to believe. I referred to the "remote-controlled victims" because that is exactly what the narcissistic abuser does—they are leading you around in circles, taking you back and forth between emotions, and alternating between bumping and backing into your thoughts. At the end of the day, the victim is left dazed and confused, and doesn't know the difference between fact and fiction. They are then left to depend on their abusers, who have no problem taking advantage of the situation.

## *The Origin of Gaslighting*

Knowing everything you know about gaslighting, it would be a good time to jump into the time portal and take a quick trip to the past. We will be traveling back in time to 1938 when "gaslighting" was first introduced to the general population. It all started with a stage play by the name of Gas Light for the British theater-goers. The stage play was adapted into a movie by the name of Gaslight in 1940 for the British public. The movie did well in the British theaters, and was later released in the United States in 1944.

The movie version features legendary actors and actresses such as Ingrid Bergman, Charles Boyer, Angela Lansbury, and Joseph Cotton. The movie is about a woman who lived with her aunt. The aunt was murdered during a robbery gone wrong—or was it a calculated murder? A decade goes by when the niece meets a man in Italy. They get married after a whirlwind romance, and return to the aunt's home to take up residence. The niece starts noticing that certain incidents are not adding up in her mind, and she believes that she is going mad. One of the incidents that occurs is that the gas lights in the house start dimming without anyone else being around. The niece doesn't realize that her aunt was murdered by her new husband, nor that all the mysterious events have been orchestrated by her deceiving husband. His ultimate goal was to make his wife believe that she was going mad and needed to be placed into an institution for her own sake. He had a greater goal in mind, and that was to search for the jewelry that was hidden in the house.

## *Under the Microscope: Identifying the Signs of Gaslighting*

Narcissistic abusers will try to manipulate people regardless of whether they are part of their circle or not. They will try their tactics on as many people as they can pull into their web of manipulation. It is more common than what we would like to believe and, because we live in a digital world, it is a trap we fall into without realizing it. I have seen content creators and influencers on various online platforms gaslight their followers. I even heard from someone who told me that they were asked whether people who share their lives online give others the right to judge them for their actions. When they responded that yes, they do believe that once anyone says, does, or posts anything online, it opens the door and windows for all 400,000 followers to have their say. Unfortunately, that was the incorrect answer and the person was blocked from all social media accounts. I do believe that the scenario that was shared about this particular influencer was a form of gaslighting. The sad reality is that they share their family life with people across the globe, and one can spot the very subtle hints of narcissism in the way they interact with their children. What is even sadder is that they don't realize that their followers, who have been in similar positions, can see what they are doing.

## *Victims of Gaslighting*

I am going to share some signs you may have heard before but never associated with narcissistic behaviors or gaslighting. These signs are so obvious that it is easy to dismiss them as being nothing more than a conversation. Some may consider the signs as poorly orchestrated movements, but it is a case of constant repetition which causes it to be an effective form of emotional abuse. You may be a victim of gaslighting when:

Someone insists that you did or said something that didn't happen.

Someone denies or refutes the memories of an event that occurred.

Someone insists that you are far too sensitive when you express your feelings about what is going on.

Someone tells others that they don't have much faith in your capabilities, how you're reacting, or the state of your mind.

Someone has no problem throwing you under the bus by changing the truth to suit them.

Someone will not entertain the idea that you are right and they are wrong; instead, they will manipulate it in such a way that you will doubt your version.

Someone is bullying you.

Someone is embarrassing you in front of others.

Someone is giving you the "death stare" by intimidating you.

Someone is using hurtful names such as *stupid*, *idiot*, or *dumb*.

Someone doesn't think twice to bring something from your past to the present to taunt you into being submissive.

### *Signs Indicating Possible Exposure to Gaslighting*

We get so wrapped up in our lives that we don't take note of any subtle changes that may or may not be happening. It is human nature to take everything we do at face value, even dismissing the subtle signs of being manipulated by our partners, colleagues, friends, or family members. You don't often know what is happening until you take a step back and see something that doesn't make sense. The wheels in your mind start turning as you try to backtrack to the exact moment where you believe the missing links may have been left behind. You may even find yourself feeling confused, overwhelmed, and doubtful of your decision-making ability.

Everything you are feeling may be an indication that you are, and have been, a victim of gaslighting. The signs to look out for are relatively common, and you may not have thought that there was anything sinister until now. What are these signs I have been alluding to? Thank you for asking, and I'm happy to share them with you. The signs may indicate that:

You may find yourself apologizing for everything—all the time.

You may think that you are messing up everything you attempt to do because you are struggling to get it right.

Your need to be perfect is overshadowed by anxiety, being overly nervous, and constantly worried that it won't meet everyone's expectations.

You lose confidence in your ability to do anything right.

Your heightened senses have you concerned that you may be too sensitive to possible criticism.

You are so focused on doing everything right that you start losing the most important person in your world—YOU.

You take the blame for everything that goes wrong, even if you were not involved.

You are constantly feeling: as if you don't or won't amount to anything, increasing frustration because you can't pinpoint your feelings, and the inability to feel any emotions.

### *Gaslighting Affects Your Behavior*

I have found some more signs which may help you identify whether you or anyone close to you is or has been a victim of gaslighting. I will be honest in saying that you may never know if you have been subjected to gaslighting until the information starts stacking up in front of you. I do think that everyone who starts questioning their sanity will start taking a closer look at their relationships with the people around them. Let's have a look at some of the signs that may indicate whether your behavior is affected by the side effects of gaslighting. Signs to look out for include:

people-pleasing by doing what others want

second-guessing yourself to ensure that you aren't offending anyone by saying or doing something inappropriately defending the person or people responsible for stealing the light from your soul

avoiding conflict with family, friends, or colleagues by making excuses, making up lies, or isolating yourself

always aware of how to articulate the words in your mind before you say them out loud so that you don't embarrass the narcissist in your midst

loss of interest in your hobbies and activities such as gardening, dancing, coffee dates with friends, or trips to the nail salon

# Gaslighting: The Guided Process Your Narcissistic Abuser Doesn't Want You to Know

This is something narcissistic abusers don't want to be mentioned because then they will know that they have been exposed. I wouldn't be truthful and caring if I didn't share the process with you. Some may even suggest that I am a narcissist, and am gaslighting my audience for fame and fortune. How wonderful it would be if it were true, but as I have previously mentioned, I have been where you are. I have crawled through the trenches of insanity and a world where my thoughts were no longer my own. I was constantly lied to and made to feel as if I was in the wrong. You can throw any scenario my way and I will tell you how it was for me. That is one of the reasons why writing this book is comforting for me, because I can share my experiences with others who are afraid to make the break. I have made it my mission in life to help people of all genders, religions, ages, and ethnicities to break the cycle of being in an abusive relationship.

Let's take a look at the seven stages involved in a narcissistic gaslighting scheme. This is how they worm and wheedle their way into the nooks and crooks of your mind. Their manipulation techniques start working as soon as they have their vision set on you. They believed that they saw a weakling who would wobble at the knees. Little do they know, but I am going to help you recognize and identify their gaslighting process. You are going to nip your gaslighting narcissist's attempts to gain control of you, in the butt. Always remember that you are the designated driver of your life.

## *Stage One: Lies and Exaggerations*

Your narcissistic abuser will openly lie to you, but behind your back they will spin their truth to make it look as if you are at fault. They don't want you to succeed in anything, and they have no shame in kicking you to the curb. They will continue smearing your reputation until you start believing that you are at fault, and that you single-handedly tainted your reputation, as well as whoever else is connected to you. All the while, the person gaslighting you is standing under the mistletoe, waiting for the praise they generated on your behalf. Remember that narcissistic gaslighting abusers have no conscience, they will lie with confidence, and they will have no problem convincing their audience that the sky is pink instead of blue.

## *Stage Two: Constant Repetition*

Narcissistic abusers have no problem using whatever tools they have available to draw you into their webs. One of the most dangerous tools, based on my opinion as well as those who have been where I was, is the larynx. This nifty little part of our body is both a blessing and a curse. Now, the reason why I view it as a curse is that narcissists will use that little voice box to manipulate their victims. Yes, it is true, because they will continue to repeat their narratives until their victims believe their repetitive verses to be true. This is one of the gaslighting tools that abusers love to use because, as I have mentioned in previous chapters, the more you hear or see something, the greater the chance is that you will see, hear, and believe it.

## *Stage Three: Chernobyl Gaslighting Event*

I want you to picture a bomb going off in the center of the city you live in. That bomb will reach the outskirts or surrounding areas, or suburbs. Now add yourself into the picture, and replace the bomb with your narcissistic abuser. You are calling your abuser out for almost all the offenses you have discovered about them. You may recall that narcissists do not like being called out, because they want to be the heroes in their life stories. As part of their gaslighting technique, they will act out in shock, horror, and disbelief because they are being made to look like the one at fault. These narcissistic abusers will retaliate, and will come at their victims with allegations, accusations, and backpedaling to throw their victims off their scent. Sadly, the victims are left standing in the center of the town, made to look like a fool for ever daring to stand up to or go against their abusers.

## *Stage Four: Mentally Defeating the Victim*

Gaslighting takes its toll on all victims of narcissistic abuse. The abusers will take whatever they can get out of their victims. They will take advantage of every situation and manipulate their victims, who are already struggling with life. Narcissistic abusers will stop at nothing to grab hold of the opportunity to break their victims down even more. The victims of these gaslighting schemes will feel discouraged, have no trust, and doubt themselves. The abusers will be watching as their victims wither and crumble under all the fear and self-doubt.

## *Stage Five: Codependency Relationships*

We have learned that narcissists want to be seen as heroes in their victims' lives. They want their victims, as well as onlookers, to believe that they are the best partners, friends, co-workers, or family members that anyone can have. In front of others, they will look like loving and supportive individuals; but, behind the scenes, the abusers want their counterparts to know that they will always be there. Narcissistic abusers want to be accepted by their victims and, slowly but surely, they will demand traction to be approved and respected by everyone. The victims, thinking nothing except that they are happy, will relinquish everything to their abusers. The narcissistic abusers, in turn, will continue gaslighting them by making thinly veiled threats insinuating that they will break up with them, fill them with fear, and prey on their vulnerability—the perfect recipe for a delightful co-dependency relationship.

## *Stage Six: Fool's Paradise*

Victims of narcissists will find themselves living in a fool's paradise where they only see good. Newsflash: narcissistic abusers want to create an illusion that all is good and well in their gaslighting world. This is manipulation central for abusers because they believe that they hold all the cards. We have learned a lot about narcissistic abusers, and we know that they will stop at nothing to make their victims feel special. They will also not give up the opportunity to swoop in to be the knight in shining armor, which is what they do in this fool's paradise. Abusers will present a facade that they are supportive by reassuring their victims that they will be there to help them if they can't do something. What they are actually telling their victims is that they can do a better job at it than the victims ever could. Living in the fool's paradise is one of the manipulation techniques used by gaslighting technicians to enforce and strengthen codependent relationships. These craft critters know what they're doing.

## *Stage Seven: Ultimate Authority*

Your narcissistic abuser is going for the all-inclusive "hole in one" when they are in the thick of their gaslighting scheme. This stage is their "hitting the big time" when they have total control over their victims. They have performed such a stellar task of taking control, dominating, and taking advantage of their victims that all inhibitions have been stripped away for the victim. The abusers are smiling and rejoicing that they have what they set out to do, which was to gaslight their victims and take away their power and ability to think and act for themselves. At the end of a very long and tiring day, the victims of these gaslighting tactics have been filled with doubt, insecurity, and fear, which is what their abusers have wanted from the start.

## *The Results of Being a Victim of Gaslighting*

The first four chapters have been filled with as much information as one could put together. All possible avenues were covered to give you a comprehensive guide as to what you, a loved one, or a colleague may be going through. We have referred to narcissists, narcissistic abusers, and people with narcissistic personality disorders. We have just added another type of narcissist to the mix—the gaslighter. No matter what they are called, or what they are addressed as they are and will remain abusers. The side effects, as implemented by gaslighters, cover the bases of all the other types of abusive methods we have been introduced to and covered. You may recall that I had high-lighted emotional abuse as being the worst, because no one can identify the residual pain left after words that cannot be retracted, have been said.

This leads us to explore what the victims of gaslighting may be experiencing. We have to remember that narcissists are very clever; they will start off slowly and build themselves up until they have spun that web tightly around their victims. The sad reality is that victims don't realize what has happened until they are cocooned in their web. I wanted to summarize the seven stages I have already covered, to give you another view of what you may be experiencing.

## *Disbelief*

I believe that narcissists walk around their victims muttering "slow and steady wins the race" under their breath. They know that everything they do has to be done slowly and consistently. They will repeat everything they want you to remember so that it sticks in your subconscious. When the victim realizes what is happening, normally when they start questioning themselves, they are left in disbelief that someone they cared for would take advantage of them. They will start noticing little things that don't seem right, and they will start asking questions, but never get the answers that seem to fit with what they are feeling. Their abusers will tell them whatever they want to hear as they reel them in with promises of trust, and whisper whatever they want to hear at that moment. It is safe to say that not all narcissistic abusers want to harm their victims. They want to be the sole focus, at all times, because they demand attention and to be the center of attention.

## *Defensive*

The victims of narcissistic gaslighting will stand up for their abusers, should anyone say anything that they don't like. It is only natural to want to protect the person who has promised that they would always be there for you, look out for you, and help you in any way you need. The abusers have done a fine job at shielding their victims from family and friends, because those that are closest will see the writing on the wall. I have seen many families who have gone through the same type of experience. One such family tried to warn their son that his girlfriend was taking advantage of him, and he became aggravated. He left his family home, only to return two years later without his girlfriend, a baby in his arms, and a mountain of debt. He said that he had woken up one night to the screaming baby, and upon investigating, the girlfriend had cleaned out her dresser and took off. His family welcomed him back, but the sad reality is that he, like many other victims, defended her and gave up his family for her. At the end of the day, he could return back to the loving arms of the family who had tried to warn him.

## *Depression*

Depression is a dark cloud that covers you when you realize that you are lost. You go through all types of motions, emotions, feelings, and anger that you want to sit in a corner and not move. Your abusers have done a number on you to the point where you don't recognize who you are. You become even more withdrawn from everyone around you because you believe that no one else believes in you. Your abuser is controlling every aspect of your life with their remote control. You are feeling physically and emotionally drained. Your abuser is in control of making all the decisions that were once your responsibility. They have taken away your dignity, and you feel worthless. This is the dark and musky place where you will be shown a play-by-play account of your past with your abuser. You don't want to be in this place. You don't deserve to be in this place. Let's get you out of here before it is too late for you to find your meadow of joy and happiness.

# Chapter 5:

# Finding Your Inner Peace

*Do not let the behavior of others destroy your inner peace.* –Dalai Lama

This is the chapter where I am going to have you run around and grab all the essentials you would find in a first aid kit. Put everything you have collected—bandages, antiseptic creams, gauze, and whatever else you would need to treat wounds—in a small basket next to you. I want you to keep them close, where you can see them, so that you can imagine the healing you will be receiving. You have been waiting for this section since you picked up this book. I've never made a promise I didn't keep, and hey, when I say I'm going to do something, I keep my word. The following four chapters are all about *YOU* and what *YOU* can do for *YOURSELF*. This is the beginning of the "*F.R.E.E. Yourself Movement*" that I have put together.

You discovered, or someone pointed out, that you were in a toxic relationship where you were being mentally, verbally, and physically abused. You didn't want to believe your gut instinct, nor the person or people who made you aware of the situation. You wanted to believe that everyone was wrong, and that your gut instinct was siding with everyone because a minute part of you believed what was being said. You were in denial, and you most likely are still in denial—even after escaping from the glass trophy case in which you were held hostage. The voice in your head was telling you what you didn't want to hear; but, as far as voices in your head go, it is difficult to ignore them because the voices get what they want, which is your attention. You started paying attention to the voices in your head, and you followed the breadcrumbs that your narcissistic abuser was leaving.

You took a step back and had a bird's-eye view of many different time frames where you were being manipulated to conform to your abuser's demands. You became aware of everyone around you giving you warnings, but they were clouded by the blinding light that your narcissist used to dominate your attention. You only had eyes for your knight in shining armor. How could you have missed those crucial moments where people who cared about you were shoved aside? How did they become shadows? Realization creeps in and the shadows become clear. The warnings are not being filtered, and your knight in shining armor is thrust into darkness. You become aware of the confusion, the hurt, the anger, and everything associated with emotions that were taken from you. You know what to do, and this is where you find yourself right now, at this very moment. You are ready to find the peace that has been buried under piles of lies, deceit, and confusion.

# It's All About Peace

I would like you to do something for me before we can move forward on this journey. Please unpack the fear you are carrying with you. I would like you to leave it right here, where it cannot hurt you again. Fear is something that you don't need in your life. Fear has a way of digging its tentacles into you, so that it can remind you of the power it holds. You will always have memories of fear, because it doesn't want you to forget what it is capable of. But, that is all it is: fear is memories that hold you back. What you want to do is to pick a couple of bunches of peace from the bushes at this entryway. Peace is stronger than fear, and guess what? Peace will help you conquer fear. So, let's drop fear, pick a couple of bunches of peace, and let's get moving.

The dictionary tells us that peace represents tranquility, when everything around you is experiencing conflict or if there is an uneasy feeling. Another entry, as given by Merriam-Webster, is that peace is a feeling of freedom from oppressive thoughts, behaviors, or actions (Merriam-Webster, 2019b). I think that peace means something different to everyone who experiences it. I like to think of peace as a little island in my mind where I can escape to. My little peace island allows me to move around without the shackles that hold me hostage. I can jump around, laugh, shout with joy, and be free before I have to return to my reality. Peace island was around when I was in the throes of my narcissistic relationship. It was there that I learned what my partner was doing to me: shielding me from my family, friends, and colleagues. I even discovered that they were hiding job offers from me. I would recommend that everyone visits their peace island for some clarity and direction. Oh, and the best thing about peace island is that no one has to know about it until you are ready to share.

## *Finding Peace Between the Layers of Fear*

I realize you may not be ready to leave your fear at the door, and that is perfectly fine. Trust is a factor we need to work on before you can find the level of peace your mind, body, and soul yearns for. I get it. I become overly excited at the thought of helping others find their peace and healing. I have to keep reminding myself that everyone has to go through a cleansing process, and they have to learn at their own pace. Nobody will ever know what you went through during your rendezvous with your narcissist, and no one may ever know. The scars you have etched into your mind and soul will only become evident to you when you start unpacking everything that has happened to you. Healing will not happen overnight. You may find yourself going through denial, and wanting to go back to your narcissist. It's time to be strong, and understand that you can have the peace you deserve.

Peace is not about you giving up on your dreams, nor is it about being submissive when you are asked by your abuser to reconsider your position. You are not responsible for how others are treating you because you have the free will to know how you want to be treated. Who are these individuals who want to take away your right to decide what you should be doing? They are no one that you would want in your circle. This little peace trip we are on is all about what you deserve as a human being. You are going to take back the power that was rudely stolen away from you. This is your life, and you are going to take back control. You are going to apply the goals to the various areas of your life that you need to build up and strengthen. We are going to manifest all these goals and powerful affirmations, taking back control and everything positive, to show this universe (and your narcissistic representatives), that you will not be frightened, silenced, or weakened.

### *Look a Little Closer at Yourself*

I recently saw a question asked by someone who was looking for ways to help a friend in an abusive relationship. I didn't think much of it until I started writing this book. I took a stroll through the archives in my mind as I revisited my relationship with my narcissistic partner. Is it difficult to find peace when you leave a narcissistic relationship or situation? Remember that narcissists and scenarios come in all types of categories, which could mean a family member, a colleague, a neighbor, or even a stranger at the store or online. How would you feel if I told you that finding peace is easier than you may think?

All I am going to require from you is an open mind and a mirror. That's all you will need as we do a little hop, a skip, and a jump into the next section of this chapter. It may be a good time to remind you that you are safe here, with me, in this book. I won't let anyone hurt, bully, judge, or condemn you for whatever you may be blaming yourself for. We're dissembling the trophy cases and relocating the ominous shadows to the far reaches of the earth. I am going to help you find your very own spotlight. Then, we are going to ensure that every broken piece of your heart and soul is fused back together, so that you can enjoy your life.

## Baby Steps Towards Inner Peace: Tips and Tools

In answer to the question of whether it is difficult to find peace when you leave a narcissistic relationship or situation; I would say that the answer depends on you. A likely scenario may involve you standing at a crossroad. You have to choose the direction you want to go. The choices you are faced with are: you live in the shadows where your narcissistic abuser has placed you, or you walk away as fast as possible without looking back. Each choice you choose to accept offers you more choices, until you have reached the place you want to be. If I were to guess what you would want, it would be the choice to be free so that you can be responsible for your choices and your life.

## *Adopting Acceptance on Your Journey to Inner Peace*

Stand in front of a mirror, and take a good, long look at yourself. Talk to yourself; break the ice as you stare at each other. Seriously though, look at the lines and contours on your face. Smile, and I promise you that the person looking back will smile back at you. I can almost guarantee that you will both be feeling pretty uncomfortable, but you'll get over it. The person looking back at you knows what is going on in your soul. The person looking back at you is where you are and have been. Everything you have been feeling, experiencing, and living—the person looking back at you has been living it as well. The person looking back at you wants you to know that healing starts with the pair of you. You may both be waiting for your narcissistic representative to apologize for the hurt, but you'll be waiting for an eternity. They'll have moved on to their next victim, and you'll have been forgotten. Accept that you can't change someone who doesn't, and won't, accept responsibility for their actions. You, yes *YOU*, have a choice. You can choose to move forward, or you can choose to allow the past to consume you. This is your life, and contrary to what your beliefs have been, you honestly *do* have a choice in determining the direction in which you can go.

I *can* tell you that the paths you choose will lead you to freedom. Someone once told me something that puts our lives into perspective: "You can't change yesterday, because it has happened, and there is nothing you can do about it. You can't do anything about tomorrow because you don't know what today will bring. The best place to be is today. You can take the memories from yesterday to lay the foundation for tomorrow, but today is a gift for you to enjoy." You have the choice to leave your narcissistic relationships in the past. Whatever happened, has happened, and all that you are left with are the memories. Those memories can only return if you allow them to, but in reality, they can't do anything to hurt you. The best Band-Aid for troublesome memories to leave you alone is to accept the peace that is being offered on a silver platter.

## *Educate Yourself on Your Journey to Inner Peace*

Learn as much as you can about narcissism.

Learn how to distinguish between "regular" people and those with narcissistic tendencies.

Equip yourself with their habits, cycles, or triggers.

Narcissism is not a subject taught in any schools. This is something you have to learn the hard way: which is either by experiencing it, or witnessing someone go through it. Your instinct is to learn as much as is humanly possible, so that you can help yourself or the person trapped in a narcissistic relationship. You know how your parents, peers, and educators told you that having an education is important—I can tell you that an education in life comes in pretty handy when you least expect it. Is there a class in school that is going to teach you about being in a relationship—whether professional, familial, or intimate—with a narcissistic person? Correct me if I'm wrong, but I can't remember any classes that helped me identify what type of person I would meet. However, I do believe that learning institutions should offer more refined lessons for people who are struggling with their self-image, which relates to life skills.

We have to remember that we live in a world that is continuously changing. What was relevant 10, 20, or 30 years ago is now considered to be part of the dinosaur age. Something that was relevant back in the day may not be useful today, but I do know of an ageless topic that should be entered into the school curriculum for everyone, regardless of their gender, age, or ethnicity. This is a subject that should be featured from pre-kindergarten to college, and even as a self-help course in the workplace. This is something that everyone, regardless of whether they want to admit it or not, will find beneficial in their daily lives. You may be ready to dive into your book to hush me so that you can find out what I'm talking about… educating yourself about how you can find peace in difficult situations.

## *Education Overview*

I wish I had listened to my gut instinct, and those who had tried to show me the neon writing on the walls. I believed it was love. I believed all of what my partner was doing was out of love for me. I would have sat through classes where I was being taught that I was special, and unique, and that I was allowed to be a person with choices. I may have joined the jeering classmates by joking about having to participate in such a class, but I would have stuck it out, knowing what I know today. I had to walk on my tiptoes across streams of eggshells during the relationship with my narcissistic abuser. I had to walk around with a backpack full of judgment, condemnation, bullying, and more loneliness than I could squeeze in.

We live in a world where we are exposed to so much negativity that translates to everything that doesn't align with the principles I was raised with. I turned around and ran away from my narcissistic abuser. I had to learn some very important lessons before I could experience inner peace. It all started with little steps which include:

setting boundaries

preparing for all types of emotions

learning who you are again

learning that it is okay to mourn the loss of a damaging relationship

understanding that you don't have a switch to turn off feelings

knowing that it is perfectly okay to put yourself and your needs ahead of others talking to others who have either been where you were, or trained therapists who can help you

These are a couple of the processes you can initiate to help you reach that place of inner peace you desire. I can promise you that your family, friends, and loved ones will understand when you tell them that you need to find yourself. They will be only too happy to have you back, when you are ready. I would like to add, as a side note, that you should try to include those you trust to help guide you back to the place where you want to be.

## **An Educated Guide to Finding Your Inner Peace**

Would you believe me if I told you that your inner peace has always been part of you? It is a place where you would go as a baby, a toddler, a busy child, a teenager, and all the way to your adult life? It is a place that offers you comfort when you are feeling weary, lonely, angry, sad, or happy. I believe that it is right here, where we need some education and guidance to build up, reinforce, and strengthen our inner peace. Education is not only about learning facts and figures; it is also about learning how to adapt and grow our skills as human beings. Have you ever watched a group of people at lunch, sitting under a tree, or playing pickleball at school? Even people watching at the mall will prove to be an educational experience.

We tend to focus on the negative aspects of human interaction, but I can promise you that not everyone will have that feeling. You don't know what a smile will do for someone you happen to see across the store. Your smile may be what someone needs, at the moment, to let them know that everything will be okay. You don't need a formal education to show someone how to find that comfort zone deep within their souls. Let's take a look at ways education may help bring the victims of narcissistic abusive relationships peace to their souls.

### *Boosting Confidence and Instilling Hope*

I replayed the strategies that helped me build my self-confidence. This was the key to finding the peace I needed to face each day. I had to learn how to get my mind working again. Part of that process was to remember my achievements from work, and my personal life which included my lovely children. I realized that the healing I was receiving was motivating me to continue reaching for my dreams and even more achievements that were waiting for me. This realization validated me as a person. It helped me forge a new path for myself. I learned how to treat myself with respect, and to live a little and pursue the dreams I am passionate about. In short, I remembered everything that made me happy, put a smile on my face, and a skip in my step as I walked.

## *Thinking Independently*

I would suggest that you pack your bags and start traveling the country, or the world, if you want to gain some independence. I wasn't going to remain in that cocoon my narcissistic partner had put me in. I packed my bags and traveled. I met and interacted with so many people. I listened to those who wanted to talk, and other times we just enjoyed sitting in silence. I realized what I had always known—I am a people person. I crave the socialization that my narcissistic partner deprived me of. I will never allow someone else to influence my thought process or decision-making ever again, because I am allowed to have an opinion. I will choose how I filter and process the information I gather through my interaction with those around me.

## *Journaling*

This is something that I have touched on at the end of Chapter 4, as we were transitioning to this chapter. I am a believer that writing down your feelings is healing. I know that writing is not everyone's cup of tea, but you are free to explore different ways to draw your thoughts out of your head. I have heard of people walking around with voice recorders, others making videos, and some more turning to online journaling websites. I can't speak for anyone else, but I like the feeling of the pen between my fingers and the paper moving under my hand as the pen meets the paper. I can write for hours, if given the chance, or I can skip a couple of days; but, I always return to my journal to help me declutter what is happening in my head.

I will share a couple of tips to help you get started on your journaling journey. You don't have to feel pressured, and you get to set the pace. I can assure you that, once you get into the swing of it, you will find self-healing and inner peace, and it will give your confidence the boost it needs to conquer the world and slay the narcissist dragon.

Think about what you would like to achieve from journaling.

Make a list of all the goals you have.

Find a place where you can be comfortable as you write down your first word.

Find a system that works for you, not for that voice trying to dictate what you should be feeling.

You may struggle with this step, but it should improve when you grow in confidence—be honest with yourself.

Don't overthink or over complicate your journaling experience—it can be as easy as riding a bicycle or as difficult as knitting a scarf.

Consider creating a routing during the initial starting process, as it will give you some structure until you are comfortable and confident to move forward, without assistance.

## *Consider Having a Support System*

Have you ever heard the proverb, "it takes a village to raise a child?" The same can be said for a support system for people from all walks of life and those struggling with illnesses, or even mental exhaustion. Everyone needs someone in their lives to boost them up or carry them, in the times when they are weary. I have seen many people walk around pretending to be all macho and buff. They say that they don't need anyone and that they are more than capable of dealing with their issues. Do we believe them? Some people may, but many don't and see straight through the bravado act they are sporting.

Being a victim in a narcissistic relationship is hard work because you are so broken down that you don't know where you're heading. It may take a moment for your mind to catch up to where you need to be, but don't give up—it will happen. You will experience moments where you will want to go back to what is familiar to you, especially when you have to deal with the constant pleading, begging, and promises, which are often followed by hints of threats, subtle threats, and very scary threats. This is where you need a support system, even if it is only one person. Remember that it takes one nail, one brick, or one grain of sand to build a house.

## *The Make-Up of a Stellar Support System*

You know that you have your village of supportive people rallying around you. You know that everyone wants to be there to help you with the recovery process. You appreciate the love and support you are receiving, but you may be feeling that you would like to connect with people who know and understand what you are going through. There seems to be a kinship among people who have experienced the same, or similar, type of abusive relationship or trauma. This is in no way, shape, or form a kick in the face to your village teammates. Your village will always be part of you, but you may need to help others who are, or have been, where you are and who are afraid to follow the healing process.

### *Meeting New People*

Meeting new people may not feature in your immediate future. All you may want right now is to rebuild the life your narcissist broke down. Where does one even go to meet new people? I have it on good authority that joining support groups is a pretty good way to meet people who have gone through trauma or abuse. Building up a support group of people who share similar experiences can help with the management of stress, fear, and anxiety. Having someone you can reach out to when you are feeling overwhelmed can prevent you from taking a stroll through the dark layers of grief.

### *Making Time to Grow Your Circle*

One of the biggest excuses we have come up with in the past couple of years is, "I don't have the time." We do tend to forget that a day only has 24 hours in it, and between work, sleep, and life, we neglect ourselves. One of the best pieces of advice that I can give you is that you need to learn how to re-organize your life to include yourself. It sounds crazy to say that you need to include yourself, but if you take a step back, how much of your day is dedicated to you going to coffee with a friend, or enjoying a beach day with a group of friends? I can give you the answer, and I will then tell you to prove that I am wrong. Set aside a couple of hours, every couple of days, to do something with your friends. Go to the local spa and have a pamper day, or go to the basketball courts and shoot some hoops. Group-related activities are guaranteed to your circle of friends, and you know, when you grow your circle of friends, your support group will expand because everyone can do with more love, life, and laughter in their daily lives.

### *Read Your Audience*

The emphasis of this section is to help you grow your support system, but what happens if someone doesn't tick all the boxes? That is something that happens, even if it is a long-time friend. I have had friendships where my friends don't want to listen to what my narcissist ex did or said, because they may not believe that they were at fault. My gut instinct was to get away from those friendships because they were still aligned with my narcissist ex. I'm not childish enough to separate my friendships into his and hers piles, because everyone has the freedom to choose who they want to be friends with. If there were conflicts of opinions, I would distance myself and not share if I was having a bad day or if I had been triggered by something. I want to say that you should trust your gut instinct 80% of the time, but the other 20% may lead you to make the wrong decisions, so think about how the situation will make you feel if you looked at it from another perspective. Trust yourself, and don't doubt the decisions you make. If you do start doubting yourself, take a break and try again another day, but don't act in haste.

# Chapter 6:

# Revering in Ultimate Freedom

*Freedom is the oxygen of the soul.* –Moshe Dayan

Welcome to the second step of the F.R.E.E. method. The first step saw you learning how to accept, invite, and embrace peace in your life. I touched on some helpful hints and tips to put you on the path of healing when leaving your narcissistic relationship. Reconnecting with your inner peace is no easy task, especially if you have experienced an abusive and traumatic relationship. The steps that were discussed, and the examples provided, have been provided by people I have met with, interviewed, and through personal experiences. What worked for me, may not work for you, and that is the beauty of sharing a variety of tips and tricks, because they can be mixed around to see what would work for you. Not everything has to, or can, go together like peanut butter and jelly, or macaroni and cheese. Maybe you would prefer to have bacon and banana on your toast, or celery sticks dipped in Nutella. It doesn't have to be a perfect combination for it to work.

The second step of this journey is all about helping you get rid of the shackles that are restricting your freedom. I feel very strongly about people being free to be the masters or mistresses of their lives. I don't like the idea of being restricted from moving, thinking, acting, or doing things you enjoy. Throughout this book, I have spoken about victims being in an invisible cage, or a trophy case, for all to gawk at. I can think of nothing more restricting than being paraded around by your narcissistic partner who allows others to criticize or judge you. You want to scream out and let everyone know that you didn't choose the outfit you are wearing or that you don't want to be there, but you are silenced by fear. That is going to end, because this chapter is going to help you break free from the shackles that are holding you back. You are going to run away from your narcissistic partner. You will no longer be smothered by their charming demeanor, their constant need to be primed, or their over-the-top criticism.

# Embracing Your Long-Awaited Freedom

I wrote down many notes when I was working on the structure for my book. I had to be sensitive, yet also firm, when explaining the scenario. The first four chapters are a testimony to what narcissists will do and what they are capable of. I know that many people are still in those relationships because they are afraid of what their abusers will do to them. Many of us have lived with the threats, the lies, the dismissive apologies that meant nothing to us, or the constant breaking down of our spirits. I know of people who are working with therapists to help them prepare for the "great escape." I also know of many people who are stuck in abusive narcissistic relationships because of the power their partners have over them. I wrote this book for those who are afraid to break free. I live in hope that everyone who finds themselves stuck in the quicksand of narcissistic abuse will read this book and know that they can walk, jump, or run as far away as they can. Help is just a call away.

Why do you need freedom from a narcissist? The answer to this question can be found in the first four chapters. Your physical, mental, and emotional health and well-being depends on you to cut those apron strings. You were never meant to be held captive by someone who doesn't value the person you are meant to be. You have as much right to freedom as the next person. Carefree comes to mind, not someone who has to fight for love, affection, and truth. We know that narcissists will stop at nothing to keep you in their line of sight, and that will include making empty promises and threats, as we have previously discussed.

## *The Essence of Freedom*

Law-abiding human beings have a right to freedom. I do say law-abiding because individuals who choose to break the law have to suffer the consequences. You did not break the law by becoming involved with a narcissist. I know that being in a relationship with a narcissist may seem like a prison sentence. I also know that you may believe that you can never be free. But, I am here to tell you that you are wrong. You can be free and experience freedom. Start believing that you can and will experience the physical, psychic, and relationship freedom you desire. These are three important types of freedom for people who find themselves in a relationship or partnership with a narcissistic individual. Are you ready to plan your prison break? All you need to remember, and keep reminding yourself, is that you have a right to experience the three most important types of freedom in any human life.

## *Prison Break: The Plan*

Start picturing your freedom. Picture yourself twirling or jumping as you feel the sun's kisses or the rain's tears of joy on your skin. The essence of freedom is so close that you can smell it, as the barriers begin to fall away. Before you can reach out and grab your freedom, you will need to plan your escape. Every prison break requires that you have a plan. The idea is to follow the plan and stick to it to ensure that you don't go back. You may have the urge to throw in the towel and return to your life the way it was. Everyone who has been in the same position you are in has wanted to give up. Many have given up, and many have stuck to their plans. I'm not going to lie and tell you that it is easy, because it's not. You will see the freedom beckoning on the horizon, but all is not as it seems. You are going to have to work to get there, such as walking barefoot across beds of egg shells, through bushes of thorns, and swimming through rivers of slime. Plans will help you avoid the egg shells, thorns, and slime.

## *Setting Boundaries*

Boundaries were created to help build protective walls between people and situations. I am a firm believer that it is essential to have boundaries in all parts of our lives. They are there to protect us from being taken advantage of, used or disrespected, or from being abused. I have spoken to many people who have told me that when their partners, friends, colleagues, or family members make them feel uncomfortable, they create an invisible barrier. If anyone would cross that barrier and enter their personal space, they would use their voice as loudly as possible, to let the "intruder" know that they have entered forbidden terrain. Boundaries are there to keep a person safe. They allow other parties to know that they need to be respected. We know that narcissists believe that certain rules don't apply to them. They feed off the fear that their victims carry around with them.

### No Bullying

Don't allow your narcissist codependent to bully you into backing down or away from what you want. Creating boundaries is something you want, and your abuser will attempt to hijack the proceedings, but you are in control. Remember that they can't hurt you because you remove yourself from their grasp. They may believe that they are still in control, but no—you are the one holding the chips, or should I say the blueprints, to your freedom. Should you feel as if you are not making any progress, you can stand up and walk away after making your point about setting boundaries.

### Demanding Respect

You have the right to demand the respect you deserve. Creating boundaries will show your abusers that you have grown a couple of inches and that you are worthy of receiving respect. Stand up straight, shoulders squared, and look those bullies in the eye as you tell them how things are going to be, and what you demand from them. Remember, they will try to hurt you, but you are building up the resistance. Isn't it wonderful to feel the power of freedom coming for you?

### Demanding Privacy

It is your right to demand privacy when stepping away from an abusive relationship. We know what narcissists are capable of, and no amount of stepping around will change the way they operate. It is part of your right to freedom that allows you to stop or prevent your narcissistic abuser from sharing details of your relationship. Some things are meant to be private, respected, and protected.

## You Are in Charge

The best piece of advice I ever received was that I was in charge when I walked away from my abusive relationship. When it came to setting boundaries, I had the upper hand over my partner because they realized that I wasn't going back for a second, third, or fourth round of deranged abuse they were freely dishing out. I realized, early on in those boundary-setting days, that I didn't have to tell my partner how I was feeling or explain what was going on in my head. I'm not going to lie and say that they didn't try to get in my head, but I wouldn't give them an inch to enter my mind palace. I felt freer than I had ever felt knowing that I was in charge of my thoughts, feelings, and emotions once again. Gone are the days that I would start a sentence with "I'm sorry, please forgive me."

## Towing the Tolerance Line

I know that it may seem overwhelming when creating boundaries between two or more parties. I promote having and setting healthy boundaries, especially where children are concerned. Children are vulnerable and are most often in the direct line of fire, which makes them feel unsafe. I believe that adults could learn a thing or two from children. Children are taught from an early age to be vigilant of what is going on around them, and that if they do not feel comfortable around someone, to speak to an authoritative figure. Adults in abusive narcissistic relationships are not always as lucky. Somewhere between being a child and becoming an adult, we lost our protective shield and we became sponges. We soaked up all the dirt and grime, as well as the love, life, and laughter that came with being adults. That is, until the scales fell from our eyes and we realized that we were experiencing the opposite of what we had learned growing up.

### *Strengthening Your Plans: Resisting Your Narcissistic Representative*

You and I know that narcissistic abusers will try any tricks in the book to get their victims under their thumbs again. We are well aware of the threats, promises, charm, and emotional and verbal abuse that will follow when they realize that none of their tactics are working. You have done a good job at building up your resistance, but you can do more to strengthen your freedom break. All it will take is one drop of self-doubt to open up a can of worms that was buried under a pile of wood in the forest. Let's look at ways in which we can strengthen our resistance walls to withstand any possible attacks from our narcissistic counterparts. Remember that we are reinforcing the boundaries we have already created to protect us and help us find the freedom we deserve.

The boundaries you have created are based on the reality and truth you want from your life after leaving the abusive relationship.

Be prepared for the counter-attacks on the boundaries you have created, because your narcissistic counterpart will take their anger out on you if they can't get what they want.

I previously mentioned that it only takes one attempt to break you down; stop enabling them by giving them a stepping stone to re-enter your life, and stop making excuses for their behavior, because this is one broken-winged chicken you cannot fix.

Distract yourself from the onslaught from your narcissistic abuser by stepping out into the community and doing something meaningful, such as volunteering at a soup kitchen or performing random acts of kindness.

Grow your support circle with good people who would rather build everyone up instead of breaking them down; narcissists love positive people when they stand alone, but they do feel threatened when the group is big and strong.

## *Prison Break: The Execution*

The plans have been drawn up, boundaries have been set, and you have worked on strengthening your boundaries. The time has come to execute your plan of action. Negotiations may have reached a stalemate, or your narcissistic representative is jumping back and forth in a last-ditch attempt to keep you hostage. Your mind has been made up, and you're ready to take your first steps outside of the trophy case where you have been put on display and preserved. I would like to share a couple more helpful pearls of wisdom to ensure that you will continue on your journey to healing, peace, and freedom.

## *Clarity*

You've made up your mind. You have taken everything from the relationship or partnership that you wanted, and you're heading out the door. You can hear the taunts behind you: "you won't have any friends;" "you'll be all alone for the rest of your life;" or "you'll be back when you realize you have nothing." Don't stop. Keep walking. Don't look back. Your future, featuring freedom, is waiting for you: a future free of ridicule, lying, cheating, disrespect, and condemnation. Remember why you wanted to leave. Always remember your decision, and don't ever doubt your reasons for leaving. Take a long, hard look at yourself in the mirror. Smile at the person looking back at you and tell them that you are proud of them for leaving.

## *Legal*

Employ the services of a legal representative. Narcissists don't like people in authority because it takes the spotlight away from them. Legal representatives will indicate that you are serious about reclaiming your freedom. You don't ever have to deal with your narcissistic representative again. Your legal representative will be your mouthpiece and buffer to support you and see that your narcissistic abuser will not make your life miserable. It is somewhere between you walking away, and a lawyer stepping in to represent you, that your narcissistic partner will realize that they are no longer in control.

### *Self-Care and Mindfulness*

The time has come for you to rejoice in your new-found freedom. I have a list a mile and a half long about everything you can do for yourself to enjoy your freedom. I doubt very much that you will need any ideas, but I'm all about giving people some helpful hints to get them started. No one, other than you, will know what you've been through to find your freedom. It is understandable if you are wary of treating yourself to something special to celebrate. Set aside one or two days a week to prioritize yourself. If you don't take care of yourself, no one else will. This is the time when you are going to rediscover yourself, and be the person you were before narcissism overshadowed your life. Put sticky notes on your mirrors, refrigerator, or wherever you can see them, and remind yourself that you are at peace and you are free.

# Chapter 7:

# Exhibiting a Wave of Self-Trust

*Self-trust is the first secret of success.* –Ralph Waldo Emerson

The third installment of your journey to reclaiming your life from a narcissist is about to commence. In this chapter, we are going to take back something that was stolen from us in a very sly and underhanded way. This is something we are born with, and it grows with the guidance, love, care, and support of those responsible for introducing us to life. It has always amazed me how easy it is to break something that took years of time and effort to build, in the matter of a blink of an eye. I am talking about self-trust, trusting others, and self-esteem.

The people who were tasked to take care of us as babies, toddlers, and children taught us how to believe that we could do anything we wanted. We were fearless children because we knew that someone would always be there if we fell, stubbed a toe, or needed a cuddle. These were the people that taught us how to love, trust, and be compassionate. I believe that it is safe to say that we were shielded from the harsh reality of the world, where people are not as protected as we would like to believe. Like a bird, you grow wings and, when they are strong enough, you get kicked out of the nest to go and explore the world.

Continuing with the analogy of the bird, we know that there could be bigger birds who will stop at nothing to harm smaller birds. We also know that birds get injured and, if they are lucky, they get rescued by someone with a caring heart that will nurse them back to health. The bird may come to rely on the warmth of the rescuer, and not want to leave to rejoin a flock. Other times, birds may want to leave their caregivers to continue with the journey they started on, but they are placed in a cage that restricts their movement. Instead of feeling the wind beneath their wings, they are losing their strength in the cage. They are on display for people to look at where they are being judged for how they look, their colors, or their mismatched tail feathers.

This whole scenario is representative of what happens in a narcissistic world. The narcissists will see themselves as the rescuers, because we know that they will swoop in, be the hero, and save the day. They will begin priming their victims, slowly but surely, by taking the trust that their victims are sharing. Unbeknown to the victims, they are falling for the heroism until suddenly they are placed in the cage—a little bit each day. The victims will start noticing small, but subtle, changes as their heroes lose their charm. They will continue playing games with the victim by manipulating the charm switch to suit them, until they are certain that they have won the game.

# Taking Back What Belongs to You

You are lucky in the sense that you have a condensed version of the narcissistic abuser's guide at your fingertips for ease of reference. You also know that a lot of the important bits of information will be repeated as subtle reminders. One such reminder is that you are stronger and more courageous than you believe. Another reminder is that narcissists are conniving and self-centered and, in their world, they are 10 feet taller than everyone else. They believe the stories they tell others, even when the stories change from day to day, but you dare not let them know that they made a mistake or point them in the right direction, they will expose you for being the one with misleading information or stories.

We know that narcissists aren't really interested in the people around them—not what they may or may not be going through. They don't care if it doesn't directly impact them, or raise them to higher standards. I mentioned a typical narcissistic comment from someone who had learned that a child had passed away and their response was, "that's too bad." Anyone with half a heart would show sympathy for the parents and family of that little one, but not this person. Someone reached out to me a couple of weeks ago to give me another bit of information to add to the basket of narcissistic responses from this specific content creator. I can say, with every fiber of honesty in my body, that it doesn't surprise me to hear about these actions or responses. This person has no problem sinking their vindictive, narcissistic teeth into people's personal lives, regardless of when it happened or whether it is relevant or not. This is a very narcissistic move, and when they are called out, they get red in the face, the pupils of the eyes are so big you can't see the iris, and the vampire teeth are oozing with venom.

Narcissists think only of themselves, and yes, they will reel you in like they are catching fish. They will make you trust them, share personal information, and promise you whatever you want to hear. The day that you don't fit in with their agendas, they will throw you under every bus they can to ensure that your image will be tainted for life. They will convince you that you are not loved, not cared for, or about, and they rob you of every bit of dignity you ever had. They will make you doubt yourself, your sanity, and your ability to do anything that involves caring for yourself. Narcissists have no issues with planting seeds of mistrust in your mind, body, and soul. They will have you believe that no one will ever trust you or your credibility. They will even have you believing that you cannot make decisions because your ability to judge yourself has been stripped away when you lost all credibility.

## *No More Dangling Carrots: Re-Claiming Me*

Don't allow your narcissistic representative to hold onto something that doesn't belong to them. Grab that stick they have over your head, break the string, rescue the carrot, and snap that stick in two as you throw it on the ground beside you. This is the first party trick you are going to participate in to reclaim control over your life. I have previously mentioned that you can't change what happened in the past. I know that parts of the past may come back and bite you on the heels. Make peace with the mistakes you made. Everyone will want to sling mud, and if they find happiness in doing this, then good on them. You put on your brave face, and own your past. People who truly care about you will stand by you, and those that don't will join the narcissistic party on the other side of the fence.

This is your journey to healing. You were a whole person who could think, act, do, and be whoever you wanted to be before your narcissistic representative decided they needed to remove you from your life of freedom. You obviously didn't know what was happening or why it was happening, but everything that was tailor-made to fit your perfect imperfections was yanked away. The party where this whole switch took place was hidden behind layers of charm, lies, grandiose, arrogance, and "I'm holier than thou" and you discovered the truth about three failed attempts at affection too late. It was at this point that you realized your gut intuition had been compromised, and you reignited the little flame. You discovered that your confidence and trust sensors were damaged and you need to get to work on realigning them. Let's take a look at some of the steps you can follow to repair the sensors.

### ReDiscover Yourself

Remember who you were before the course of your life was altered. Find out who is hidden beneath the layers of self-doubt, anxiety, and whatever lies you have been fed to believe. The person that was once bursting with confidence is cowering behind a wall, and is waiting to be released. Find that person, nurse them back to strength as you remember all you were before your wings were clipped.

### Be Who You Are Meant to Be

You don't have to be afraid. The cage has been opened, and you are free to fly. You can take as much time as you need to acclimatize to the normality of life. Remember that I told you that there are no shortcuts when it comes to healing. Adopt a self-care routine where you meditate, breathe, and get to know yourself until you are ready to re-enter your world. Baby steps.

### Reach Out to Your Support System

I would like to refer you to Chapter 5, where I highlighted the importance of building a support system. Having it come up in this chapter will prove to all victims that it is essential to have someone, or a group of people, they can count on to help them. Don't underestimate the power of having a system that wants to be there for you in your darkest hours. Can you imagine how relieved they must be to have you return to your life, an injured but recovering soul? It is not their fault, nor yours, that a rift was caused; but, don't allow the rift to be created again.

## *Additional Helpful Advice*

Your narcissistic partner robbed you of more than you may realize, and you may remember chunks or tidbits as time goes by, or you may not remember much at all. Remember that everything that is mentioned is only a fraction of what is out there for you to add to your toolbelt. Some additions for this section include:

being truthful about the situation you were in—don't embellish on what happened to make it more dramatic than it was (memories have a way of returning and you don't want to be in the same position as your narcissistic partner)

not being afraid to take a step back, if and when you need some room to breathe or when you need some time to reflect

setting goals, as previously mentioned, to help you regain what has been lost

creating a list of attainable but realistic goals, over a reasonable time frame

journaling to help boost your confidence and build up your trust receptacles

## *Show Yourself Some Mercy and Kindness*

I sent out an email to all the people I had spoken to during the time I was plotting and planning this book. I asked many questions, and I got additional information that I had never thought about. A couple of the people told me that I needed to include it somewhere in this book that victims are allowed to break down, be angry, or even want to give up. These people also told me that self-care is something that starts with the person reading these words. It has been mentioned many times that you can't change the past, so really, there is no point in being angry at something that has happened. You may not ever be ready to forget the past, but it would be really helpful to your overall emotional and mental well-being if you were to forgive what has happened. Please don't misunderstand me—I am not telling you to go to the abuser, nor am I telling you to get in contact with them—but I am going to tell you that you can forgive the situation without their knowledge. This is one of the most helpful and kindest things you could ever do for yourself.

It is one of the hardest things I had to learn when I left my narcissistic relationship. I was consumed with self-loathing and I didn't know how to love myself, let alone others. I had been deprived of love and filled with hatred because I had believed that I was the one at fault. It took a very long time for everything to sink in and hit home. I wasn't to blame. I wasn't the one who was lying. I wasn't the one keeping secrets from me. That is when I learned that I didn't have to be a victim of myself. I was allowed to laugh. I was allowed to have friends. I was allowed to go out and enjoy time with family and friends—my support system. I knew I was going to be okay because I wasn't the enemy.

Be kind to yourself.

Be angry if you must, but forgive yourself afterward.

You can do whatever you like doing—you don't need anyone's approval.

Remember the values you had when you started on your own—recall, reimplement, and reinforce them today.

Human beings don't have wings or propellers—the best place for you is on the ground where your feet are planted firmly.

Show yourself some love and compassion, and hug yourself every once in a while.

## *Learning the Act of Self-Love and Self-Appreciation*

Self-love and self-appreciation is something that victims of narcissistic abusive relationships struggle with. You have been broken down, stripped of so many of your unique traits, and left to fend for yourself once the ultimate task has been achieved. Our abusers have stripped us of everything we had once been proud of because they saw our traits as threats. Those who have escaped from the clutches of their narcissistic abusers have to revert to being babies in the developmental stages of their lives again. The victims of narcissistic abusive relationships have to learn to rediscover themselves. Think about someone who has suffered a traumatic brain injury and now they have to learn how to crawl, walk, and talk again. They have to learn what they liked to do, what type of food they liked, or what music and television shows they enjoyed.

Take time to become reacquainted with yourself. Many people may laugh at the suggestion, but victims of abusive relationships know what it means to come back from the brink. It is a place where no one deserves to be, and it is a place you wouldn't wish on your worst enemy. Take all the time you need to put yourself back together. You have many different options that you could utilize. Healing is a slow and steady recovery process, and it can involve anything that you enjoy. Let's have a look at some ways in which you can find yourself, boost your confidence, and learn to trust the person who has walked away from an abusive relationship.

Practice the art of meditation or yoga.

Share your thoughts and feelings in your journal, or start a blog.

Work on reaching the goals you have set up for yourself, and incorporate some new habits into your life, while eliminating redundant habits that no longer fit in with your current lifestyle.

Concentrate on your emotions, and focus on working through the emotions as they crop up.

Never be afraid to spend time doing things that make you happy; men can enjoy a grooming session at the local barber shop or have their cars detailed, and women can go to the salon for a well-deserved pamper session, or go shopping.

You don't have to be afraid to put yourself ahead of someone or something else, and you don't ever have to fight for a place in the spotlight.

Confident people act on instinct and don't think about articulating what they mean to do or say—stop trying to overthink something simple.

Allow yourself to dream about crossing the finish line and being handed the ribbon for completion—don't ever doubt yourself again.

There is more to life than wanting to be perfect at everything—embrace your perfect imperfections and flaunt them around for everyone to see.

# Chapter 8:
# Experiencing the Final Closure

*Closure happens right after you accept that letting go and moving on is more important than projecting a fantasy of how the relationship could have been.* –Sylvester McNutt

Welcome to the fourth and final installment of my F.R.E.E. method, where you have been learning how to cleanse yourself from the narcissistic residue you have accumulated. It's been a wild ride, filled with what some may say is way too much information, and others may say that there could be more. One of the toughest lessons I had to learn was that I couldn't, and can't, please everyone. It is part of the recovery process which has been mentioned multiple times throughout our journey together. You are not here, on this Earth or in this place, to keep everyone happy. What may put a smile on one person's face may ignite a frown or a scowl on someone else. It is not your job, my job, or that of the person reading this to keep you happy. That doesn't mean I won't try my best, but hey, I'm human; I make mistakes and I have errors in judgment at times, too. Guess what? I'm not perfect, neither are you, nor is the actor or actress you are crushing on.

The fourth and final installment of my F.R.E.E. method is about closing doors and moving past the pain of being in a toxic relationship. I'm not going to tell you that it is going to be easy, nor am I going to say that you will get over it. I would be exactly like the narcissist you are breaking away from. I could tell you anything you want to hear to help you justify the decision or choice you are making. I can tell you everything you need from me, but lies are a strange cumulation of words that always—without a doubt—find a way to come back and bite you on the butt. I don't know about anyone else, but I was taught by my peers that honesty is the best policy—always!

You have gone through many dark jungles to get to where you are now. You have accomplished something you had thought was lost to you forever. The only obstacle preventing you from moving forward is the foot that is preventing the door from closing. That door is the gateway between your past and your future, and the present is not wanting to let go, yet. The present is an indication that either party is holding onto something such as hope, fear, or uncertainty. I can assure you that you are not the first, nor will you be the last, victim of narcissism to hold onto something. No one ever said that you didn't love your narcissistic partner or care about a narcissistic colleague. Your feelings will always be there, but the realization is that you won't know if the feelings shared were real or make-believe.

# All Obstacles Out of the Way: Impending Closure of a Relationship

I have mentioned the foot preventing the door from closing on a chapter that has reached a stalemate. All that the chapter needs is a conclusion with the words "the end" and a period to indicate finality. Is it possible to get the closure you want and need following your exit from your narcissistic partner's clutches? This is an answer that many will weigh in on, but the ultimate answer will come from the three people in the relationship: the victim, the abuser, and the partner. Yes, I said three people, because the victim sees their partner as two different people—the one they got to know before their true colors presented themselves and the real person they now know them to be. Each relationship is different and may involve both parties, where they may have shared assets, investments, pets, or even children. Walking away may prove to be easier said than done, but a narcissist would and could use those shared interests to their advantage.

What happens if the relationship is void of attachments? Great question, and I would love to discuss this with you. Closure is difficult, and it doesn't matter whether it was a mutual decision, one-sided, or one that was forcibly terminated. The fact remains that whether you are or were in a relationship where real feelings were a factor, closing the door is going to be tough. However, we are here to discuss the termination of a narcissistic relationship, and what closure may look like for the victim. This section of this chapter is not to be seen as a regression in healing. You are here to learn about the finer details that you may have missed when tiptoeing, walking, or running away from your abuser. We are tying up loose ends, and ensuring that your first aid kit has everything it needs to help you find what you have missed out on.

## *Oh No, You Aren't Going Anywhere— Regards, Your Narcissist*

Don't be afraid, don't show your fear, and don't allow this intimidation tactic to grab hold of your sensors. This little section is not going to put a halt to your "freedom" campaign. You are going to get what you want, and you are going to slay the dragons your narcissistic partner is sending out after you. At the end of a very long mud-slinging contest, they are losing their prized possession—*YOU*! They will attempt to grasp at all straws to ensure that they don't lose you, but the reality is that they lost you the very first day that they decided to put you in the trophy case. Stand behind me, and I will protect you. I've been here, so I know all the tricks that they will have up their sleeves. Always remember that you have made that all-important decision to break ties. Anything that you will hear from your abuser is hot air as they realize that you can see through their charm.

## *It's All About Them*

One of the first traits we mentioned was that everything had to revolve around the narcissist. They were and are the most important figure in the equation. They see themselves as superior and cannot imagine what it would feel like to have the tables turned. Oh, they see you, your tears, your pain, your anguish, and your anger; but it doesn't bother them as much as it would you. When you walk away, they aren't pining over you leaving them; they are concerned about who they are going to feed off when their supply and demand have been removed. You have to do what is right for you, and no one can make the decisions for you. You have been on the other side of the trophy case, you know what your narcissistic abuser was capable of, and you are at the crossroads deciding which is the best way forward for you.

## *They Don't Want to Let Go*

I have mentioned that narcissists are not concerned about losing their partners. They are concerned about their image and who is going to shine their halos, going forward. They will stop at nothing to reel you back into their web. *No* is a word they don't know or understand. It is foreign to them because no one has ever used it. Now, they are faced with the most heinous foreign crimes, which include their "loving" partners leaving them. They will pull out all the cards in their narcissistic deck to get their victims back. One of the most commonly used excuses to not let go is when they will tell you that they need time to think and come up with a solution. Just be aware that those negotiations can be stretched out further than an elastic band.

## *Closure in the Eyes of a Narcissist*

This is an interesting one that I believe many victims of abuse are caught up in. Narcissists, as we know, are conniving and cunning, and they are skilled at the games they play. I am almost convinced that they have a vault hidden somewhere that is holding the playbooks and awards that they have won. Narcissistic abusers know how to turn those tables upside down to make themselves look like the victims in any scenario. They will milk their version of the closure of the relationship for more than it's worth. I can confidently say that their version will make the actual victim seem as if the abuser is a saint. You know what the truth is, so don't back down. Walk away with the pride and dignity that you fought to reclaim.

## *Spine Straight, Shoulders Square, Turn, and Walk Away*

Everyone has their own unique version of dealing with closure. It is true that not everyone who goes through a breakup, a divorce, or a break in partnership is in some or other type of narcissistic relationship. Going your separate ways is something that cuts deep into the hearts and souls of those involved. I would like to leave you with some solid advice that I was given when I left my narcissistic relationship with my most treasured possessions. I did what I did for them because I knew that they needed a person who was whole and was not afraid of shadows. One of the people I interviewed told me that they had to put on their big kid underwear once they decided to leave their narcissistic relationship. They were dealing with a whole lot more resistance than I mentioned in the previous section. Their partner had launched a smear campaign and made up new lies with each passing day. The abuse continued and the victim just went on their merry way, knowing that fighting back would be a futile attempt. People had to make their own choices, and even when the abuser continued playing sympathy card after sympathy card, the victim went about their day with a smile on their face. They knew the truth, and that was all that mattered.

Closure begins with the person walking away. You have to be prepared for the backlash or fallout. You have the same friends, hang out in the same circles, and the chances are pretty high that what you are doing will reach your partner and vice versa. I have touched on it many times, and I will say it again: you are not at fault for leaving a toxic relationship. Your emotional, mental, and physical health is more important than being in a place where you are not allowed the freedom to be who you are meant to be. I want to leave you with a list of guilt-free and non-judgmental ways for you to walk away from a narcissistic relationship. This is not about your abuser, nor is this about friends or family. I am going to give you permission—not that you need it from me—but I want you to shrug your shoulders and count to ten as you walk away. You were not put on this earth to please other people. Always remember that whenever you are feeling guilty.

You are not your narcissistic abusers' keeper, and you can't make them do something they don't want to do.

Accept that you may never get the closure you want, and that it is perfectly fine because you are going to take each day as it appears when you open your eyes in the morning.

Make peace with the decision you have made, and remember why you did what you did—this is not about your abuser, friends, family, or colleagues—this is your totem pole and you can climb to the top.

Consider employing the services of a legal representative to act as the buffer between you and your abuser.

Don't make the mistake of stalking your narcissistic abuser on social media platforms, driving past their home, or holding onto keepsakes—make a clean break, hire a lawyer, and know that they can look after themselves—your job as the housemaid has been terminated.

## *Mourn the Demise of Your Relationship*

This is not a joke. I have seen far too many people jump from one relationship to another because they don't want to be alone. You left your narcissistic relationship because you felt trapped, you were stripped of your dignity, you were lied to, you were cheated on, and you were someone else's doormat. Take some time to reflect on what you have been through. Don't put a timeframe on this process, because you don't know when the grief and emotions will catch up with you. I have been there, remember? I left with my children. I had to be strong for them, but I had an amazing support system. I had to go through the stages of grief, and they didn't happen in any specific order. One moment I would be fine, and the next I would be angry; or, I would be laughing at something I found funny, and the next moment I would be sobbing on the floor. Trust me when I tell you that you don't want to be in a relationship with someone when you are trying to find yourself.

Guess what? I have it on excellent authority that mourning or grieving your past relationship is healing for the broken heart and shattered soul. It will put a lot of what you experienced with your narcissistic partner into perspective, and it will build you up (and triple boost your confidence). I would like to share some of the stages of grief with you. Let's take a look at what the grieving process would look like for you.

You can't believe that you ended your relationship, and you are struggling to understand why you would do it.

The memories you share with your narcissistic partner fills you with anger because you really cared about them, but they betrayed you.

You start a mudslinging battle between yourself and the narcissist—in your mind—and you are trying to find a reason or some type of common ground where everything started to fall apart; this is the stage where you may be tempted to reach out to your abuser to beg for reconciliation.

Reality starts sinking in, and you realize that to return to the unloving arms of a narcissistic abuser is going to do more harm than good, and you start feeling down in the dumps—which leads you down the very dark rabbit hole of depression.

With the help of a therapist or your support group, you begin to accept everything that has happened, what you have been through, and you realize that the only way to heal is to accept what has happened, send a silent "I forgive you" off into the universe and live your life.

### *Coping With Relationship Grief*

You are now armed with the stages of grief following your exit from your narcissistic relationship. You know what the signs are, and you know what to look out for. It is important to follow the stages of grief, and not give up. I know the temptation will be knocking on your door, but you have to be strong—for your sake, and for those who care about you. The next list I would like to share with you is something that has been mentioned and touched on throughout this journey, but it is going to receive its very own bullet-pointed list for ease of access. Remember that grief is real. The emotions that accompany grief do tap into your energy, which is why you should take your time before "getting back in the saddle." If you need to be in a relationship, have one with yourself. Prioritize yourself, and get to know the person that has been screaming for attention and affection for a very long time. That is the person you want in your corner before you go out and meet someone else.

Turn on the breaks for a bit before embarking on another relationship.

Get to know the most important person in your life—YOU!

Adopt a hobby to help you deal with your break-up.

Form new habits, and lay old ones to rest.

Allow all the mother hens in your life to cluck around you—it's okay to rely on others for support.

Consider therapy—speaking to someone other than friends and family may help you more than you think, because the therapist doesn't know your abuser.

## *Self-Healing Coping Strategies*

When somebody tells you that you need to prioritize yourself, you tend to scoff and say that you don't have enough hours in the day. When multiple people, family members, friends, colleagues, therapists, and strangers tell you to prioritize yourself, you know that you have to listen. You don't know me, and I don't know you, but we do have something in common—turning our backs on narcissistic relationships. I may have mentioned it previously, but taking care of yourself is not some form of reverse narcissism. You are allowed to be selfish when it comes to your overall mental, emotional, and physical health and well-being. Practice patience during this grieving process, and listen to what your mind, body, and soul is telling you. What can you do to place yourself on a pedestal after everyone else has been cared for? Let's take a look at some very helpful leads that will most likely ignite the spark that is needed to help you over the hurdles to find the closure you deserve.

Incorporate the practice of mindfulness into your daily routines such as yoga, meditation, dancing, or journaling.

This may be a hard one to swallow, but accept that you are not a superhero to anyone else except those in your support system—you don't have to save the world, you only have to save yourself.

Hit the pause button every once in a while, and enjoy the moment you are in; the world and its drama will still be there when you step onto the roller coaster after a well-deserved breather.

You are allowed to have an "off" day, and you are allowed to mourn for the life you had, because trauma is something that you have to work through—it won't disappear overnight.

Work on your listening skills; listen to people around you and listen to the voice in your head that is trying to get your attention.

## *The Final Closure: Crossing the Last Hurdle*

I was reading through Chapters 5, 6, 7, and 8, and realized that it was missing something. I have shared as much relevant information as I could squeeze in here, added in personal stories courtesy of my experiences, and tossed in a couple more from people I met throughout the planning and writing stages of this book. One would think that there would be some sort of confetti bomb as you turn the page to celebrate the end. I am hesitant to see this final chapter as some sort of celebration because of the emotions involved.

It doesn't matter whether you lose a loved one by death or by breaking ties with them; closure is an emotional experience. I have shared many different methods which would help you find the closure you need. I've repeatedly let you know that no two people will experience the same results or effects, and everything you do is by trial and error. Use the tools that have been shared with you, and tweak them to benefit you. Create something unique that works for you, which you can share with others. My F.R.E.E. method is something that I put together to help me find my way back to reality. I had to come back for my children, and as I told my publisher, I have moved on with my life.

I found an article written by Kenny Weiss: a life coach, speaker, and mentor. The article is titled "How To Get Closure From A Narcissist" and gives a list of most of what I have mentioned or discussed. I glanced through the article and one of the sub-headings caught my eye. I stopped, read it once (and then a couple more times), and realized that this needed to be mentioned in the final chapter.

### *The 90/10 Rule*

What is the 90/10 rule?

How does the 90/10 rule work?

How can the 90/10 rule help you find closure?

These are some of the questions my publisher wrote down, and I will attempt to answer them as concisely as possible with the help of Kenny Weiss. What we have learned from reading this book is that narcissists dominate their victims' attention. Narcissists need to have their egos stroked multiple times a day so that they can continue their tirade of manipulation. Weiss has put a ratio on narcissistic relationships which, when looking at the context it is used in, puts everything into perspective. Weiss notes that a narcissistic relationship demands that 90% of yourself belong to the narcissist, and 10% belongs to you. The representation is wholly accurate because narcissists don't like sharing, and if they knew that they are missing out on 10%, they would set all kinds of traps to ensure they get it. Weiss explains that the ratio, as it is, indicates that victims are "severely codependent" and that the dynamics need to change.

The conclusion of this informative 90/10 rule is a reminder that victims need to learn that it is perfectly okay, acceptable, and expected to love and care for themselves. Weiss wants the victims of narcissistic relationships to flip the 90/10 ratio on its belly. You should be spending 90% of your time focusing on everything YOU need for healing from your abusive relationship. Remember that YOU are the most important person (Weiss, 2021).

# Conclusion

It is hard to believe that we have reached the end of our journey together. This was a tough journey. I do believe that you have a broader understanding of what narcissism is, and what narcissistic personality disorder entails. I have given you as much information as you can squeeze into words, but I am confident that I have given you everything you could need. You have a toolkit jam-packed with everything you need to help yourself and others who may be in a narcissistic relationship.

If you want to take away one thing from this book, I would say that you should know that you are not to blame for your narcissistic partner. This is not a reflection on the person you are. Narcissism is a sick game that can, and will, be played by anyone who ticks the boxes of everything you have learned throughout this book. Anyone can turn on the charm, but only narcissists can keep that light shining for as long as they need it. I don't want you going out and thinking that everyone who smiles at you, or tries to charm you, is a narcissist—that will drive you insane. Use the tips and tricks you were given and learn to trust yourself.

I set out to help people identify if they were in narcissistic relationships. I wanted to show you that you have options, and that you don't have to stay in a box if you don't want or need to. I have seen so many wounded people, during my own healing and recovery, that my heart tore a little each time. I like seeing people smile because it reminds me that there is hope. I like seeing the sparkle in people's eyes because it lights up their faces. I believe that I have achieved the goals I set out to accomplish when I wrote this book.

# Thank You

Thank you for joining me on this journey. I hope that you have found this book as helpful and healing as I intended it to be. I would love it if you could leave a review and let me know how your life has been affected by a narcissistic relationship. I am pretty sure that other readers would like to learn from all our experiences. At the end of the day, we are united by people who set out to stunt our ability to grow as individuals, remove our voices, and rob us of our independence.

Again, thank you for joining me on this journey. Please take care of yourself, and know that help is just a click away. Until we meet again—in my next book—*See You Later*.

# References

*A quote by Moshe Dayan.* (n.d.). Goodreads. https://www.goodreads.com/quotes/1923576-freedom-is-the-oxygen-of-the-soul

*A quote by Ralph Waldo Emerson.* (n.d.). Goodreads. https://www.goodreads.com/quotes/569686-self-trust-is-the-first-secret-of-success

*A quote by Shahida Arabi.* (n.d.). Goodreads. https://www.goodreads.com/author/quotes/2980385.Shahida_Arabi

Allen, N. (2021, September 25). *This is what narcissistic abuse looks like — and why it's so harmful.* Mindbodygreen. https://www.mindbodygreen.com/articles/narcissistic-abuse-15-signs-and-warnings-to-look-out-for/

Anastasia, B. (2017, January 23). *An unsolicited suggestion: Educate yourself about the narcissistic cycle.* Medium. https://medium.com/@XLR8EDLiving/an-unsolicited-suggestion-educate-yourself-about-the-narcissistic-cycle-6cf45d1c1806

Anwar, B. (2022, February 4). *How to set boundaries with a "narcissist."* Talkspace.

https://www.talkspace.com/blog/how-to-set-boundaries-with-a-narcissist/

Atkinson, A. (n.d.). *Finding peace during challenging times with the narcissist*. QueenBeeing. https://queenbeeing.com/finding-peace-during-challenging-times-with-the-narcissist/

Barkley, S. (2022, March 1). *15 Quotes for closure after a relationship*. Power of Positivity. https://www.powerofpositivity.com/closure-after-relationship-quotes/

Bottaro, A. (2022, January 6). *6 Signs of verbal abuse you need to know*. Verywell Health. https://www.verywellhealth.com/what-is-verbal-abuse-examples-signs-and-more-5210954

Bunch, E. (2021, March 22). *Decisiveness is a learned trait—here are 11 tips to master the art of decision-making*. Well+Good. https://www.wellandgood.com/how-to-be-more-decisive/

Cambrell, A. (2021, June 7). *Relationship grief – 5 powerful steps to get through it*. Counseling in Melbourne. https://www.counsellinginmelbourne.com.au/relationship-grief/

Capecchi, S. (2022, January 5). *Emotional abuse: Signs, types, & how to deal with it*. Choosing Therapy. https://www.choosingtherapy.com/emotional-abuse/

Christian, L. (2021, March 22). *How to be your authentic self: 7 Powerful strategies to be true*. SoulSalt. https://soulsalt.com/how-to-be-your-authentic-self/

Cirino, E. (2018, July 19). *6 Ways to build trust in yourself*. Healthline. https://www.healthline.com/health/trusting-yourself

Cleveland Clinic. (2019, January 16). *7 Tips for better patience*. https://health.clevelandclinic.org/7-tips-for-better-patience-yes-youll-need-to-practice/

Cleveland Clinic. (2020, June 19). *Narcissistic personality disorder*. https://my.clevelandclinic.org/health/diseases/9742-narcissistic-personality-disorder

Cohen, S. E. (2022, June 22). *How do you get over a narcissist & get your self-esteem back?* Sandra Cohen PhD. https://sandracohenphd.com/how-do-you-get-over-a-narcissist/

Cunha, J. P. (2020, August 10). *What are the nine traits of a narcissist?* EMedicineHealth. https://www.emedicinehealth.com/what_are_the_nine_traits_of_a_narcissist/article_em.htm

David, S. (2020, February 21). *How to be kinder to yourself*. Ideas.ted.com. https://ideas.ted.com/how-to-be-kinder-to-yourself-self-compassion/

*Dealing with narcissistic abuse - a true story*. (2020, August 10). Daya, Inc. https://www.dayahouston.org/post/dealing-with-narcissistic-abuse-a-true-story

Duignan, B. (2020). Gaslighting. In *Encyclopædia Britannica*. https://www.britannica.com/topic/gaslighting

*Effects of physical abuse*. (n.d.). Nursing Home Abuse Guide. https://www.nursinghomeabuseguide.org/physical-abuse/effects

Ellis, M. E. (2019, March 27). *The real cost of untreated mental illness in America*. Constellation Behavioral Health. https://www.constellationbehavioralhealth.com/blog/the-real-cost-of-untreated-mental-illness-in-america/

Evans, M. T. (2019, January 20). *Peace after narcissistic abuse is possible*. Narcissism Recovery and Relationships Blog. https://blog.melanietoniaevans.com/peace-after-narcissistic-abuse-is-possible/

Evans, M. T. (n.d.). *Why learning everything about narcissism is not the answer*. Melanie Tonia Evans. https://blog.melanietoniaevans.com/why-learning-everything-about-narcissism-is-not-the-answer/

Exploring Your Mind. (2022, March 27). *The seven stages of gaslighting in a relationship.* https://exploringyourmind.com/stages-of-gaslighting-in-a-relationship/

Fernley, J. (2020, September 9). *How to start a journal and find inner peace.* GRateLife. https://gratelife.rate.com/how-to-start-a-journal-and-find-inner-peace/

Fjelstad, M. (2017, September 5). *15 Signs you're dealing with a narcissist.* MindBodyGreen. https://www.mindbodygreen.com/articles/14-signs-of-narcissism

GFIT Wellness. (2021, June 14). *7 Stages of gaslighting in a relationship and how to respond.* https://www.gfitwellness.ca/blog/7-stages-of-gaslighting-in-a-relationship-and-how-to-respond

Gordon, S. (2022, February 13). *How to recognize verbal abuse and bullying.* Verywell Mind; Verywellmind. https://www.verywellmind.com/how-to-recognize-verbal-abuse-bullying-4154087

Greenberg, E. (2021, February 13). *7 Myths about narcissistic personality disorder and why they're false.* Psychology Today. https://www.psychologytoday.com/us/blog/understanding-narcissism/202102/7-myths-about-narcissistic-personality-disorder-and-why-theyre

Hall, J. L. (2020, April 14). *8 Dangerous myths about narcissistic abuse.* Psychology Today. https://www.psychologytoday.com/us/blog/the-narcissist-in-your-life/202004/8-dangerous-myths-about-narcissistic-abuse

Hall, N. (2022, June 1). *Narcissistic personality disorder: Meaning, traits, causes.* Man of Many. https://manofmany.com/lifestyle/sex-dating/narcissistic-personality-disorder

Heger, E. (2022, April 26). *6 Subtle signs that you've experienced emotional abuse by a narcissist.* Insider. https://www.insider.com/guides/health/mental-health/narcissistic-abuse

Hilton Andersen, C. (2021, February 10). *15 Narcissist quotes that will help you deal with the narcissist in your life.* The Healthy. https://www.thehealthy.com/mental-health/narcissist-quotes/

Hochenberger, K. L. (2020, May 23). *Reclaiming yourself from a narcissist.* Psychology Today. https://www.psychologytoday.com/intl/blog/love-in-the-age-narcissism/202005/reclaiming-yourself-narcissist

Hogan, L. (2021, August 25). *How to be kind to yourself.* WebMD. https://www.webmd.com/balance/features/how-to-be-kind-to-yourself

Holly, K. J. (2011, May 8). *The signs of verbal abuse.* HealthyPlace. https://www.healthyplace.com/blogs/verbalabuseinrelationships/2011/05/how-to-stop-verbal-abuse-part-6-wrap-up

Hupp, N. (2020, January 13). *The power of patience: 5 Ways to develop patience.* EMindful. https://emindful.com/2020/01/13/developing-patience/

Itani, O. (2020, January 29). *Solitude: The importance and benefits of spending time alone.* Personal Growth. https://www.omaritani.com/blog/spending-time-alone

Kjærvik, S. L., & Bushman, B. J. (2021). The link between narcissism and aggression: A meta-analytic review. *Psychological Bulletin, 147*(5), 477–503. https://doi.org/10.1037/bul0000323

Kramer, B. C. (2016, September 11). *How to break free from a narcissist in 5 steps.* HuffPost. https://www.huffpost.com/entry/5-steps-to-breaking-free-from-narcissist_b_8073918

Legg, T. J.. (2020, January 2). *Narcissistic personality disorder.* Healthline. https://www.healthline.com/health/narcissistic-personality-disorder

Loggins, B. (2021, November 22). *Healing after narcissistic abuse: What does healing look like?* Verywell Mind.

https://www.verywellmind.com/stages-of-healing-after-narcissistic-abuse-5207997

Louis de Canonville, C. (2018, December 21). *What is gaslighting? | The effects of gaslighting on victims of.* The Roadshow for Therapists. https://narcissisticbehavior.net/the-effects-of-gaslighting-in-narcissistic-victim-syndrome/

Lucid Content Team. (n.d.). *The Ultimate goal setting process: 7 Steps to creating better goals.* Lucidchart. https://www.lucidchart.com/blog/the-ultimate-goal-setting-process-in-7-steps

Lynn, R. (2020, September 12). *Is journaling the key to inner peace?.* Harper's Bazaar Arabia. https://www.harpersbazaararabia.com/culture/people/is-journaling-the-key-to-inner-peace

Mathews, L. (2021, September 15). *Freedom in relationships – What it means and what it doesn't.* Bonobology. https://www.bonobology.com/freedom-in-relationships/

Mayo Clinic Staff. (2017, November 18). *Narcissistic personality disorder - Symptoms and causes.* Mayo Clinic. https://www.mayoclinic.org/diseases-conditions/narcissistic-personality-disorder/symptoms-causes/syc-20366662

MedCircle. (2020, November 10). *Narcissistic abuse: What it looks like and what to do.*

https://medcircle.com/articles/narcissistic-abuse/

Mental Illness Policy Org. (2019, January 23). *About 50% of individuals with severe psychiatric disorders (3.5 million) are receiving no treatment.* https://mentalillnesspolicy.org/consequences/percentage-mentally-ill-untreated.html

Mentzou, M. (2021, April 30). *How to break free from the narcissist cycle.* The Good Men Project. https://goodmenproject.com/featured-content/how-to-break-free-from-the-narcissist-cycle/

Merriam-Webster. (2018). Mythology. In *Merriam-Webster.com dictionary*. Retrieved July 5, 2022, from https://www.merriam-webster.com/dictionary/mythology

Merriam-Webster. (2019a). Abuse. In *Merriam-Webster.com dictionary*. Retrieved July 5, 2022, from https://www.merriam-webster.com/dictionary/abuse

Merriam-Webster. (2019b). Peace. In *Merriam-Webster.com dictionary*. Retrieved July 5, 2022, from https://www.merriam-webster.com/dictionary/peace

Merriam-Webster. (n.d.-a). Gaslighting. In *Merriam-Webster.com dictionary*. Retrieved July 5, 2022, from https://www.merriam-webster.com/dictionary/gaslighting

Merriam-Webster. (n.d.-b). Narcissistic. In *Merriam-Webster.com dictionary*. Retrieved July 5, 2022, from https://www.merriam-webster.com/dictionary/narcissistic

Milstead, K. (2021, February 4). *7 Reasons why narcissists won't give you closure.* Fairy Tale Shadows. https://fairytaleshadows.com/seven-reasons-why-narcissists-wont-give-you-closure/

Morris, S. Y., & Raypole, C. (2021, November 24). *Gaslighting: Signs and tips for seeking help.* Healthline. https://www.healthline.com/health/gaslighting

Neo, P. (2020, January 29). *What it's really like to break up with a narcissist.* MindBodyGreen. https://www.mindbodygreen.com/0-27078/what-its-really-like-to-break-up-with-a-narcissist.html

Neuharth, D. (2017, August 15). *25 Spot-on quotations about narcissism.* Psych Central. https://psychcentral.com/blog/narcissism-decoded/2017/08/25-spot-on-quotations-about-narcissism#2

Neuharth, D. (2020, June 30). *7 Ways to set boundaries with narcissists.* Psychology Today. https://www.psychologytoday.com/us/blog/n

arcissism-demystified/202006/7-ways-set-boundaries-narcissists

Ni, P. (2017, April 30). *7 Stages of gaslighting in a relationship*. Psychology Today. https://www.psychologytoday.com/us/blog/communication-success/201704/7-stages-gaslighting-in-relationship

Patricia. (2021, August 20). *12 Myths about narcissism debunked*. Inner Toxic Relief. https://innertoxicrelief.com/myths-about-narcissism-debunked/

Petersen, L. (2022, May 22). *What is the connection between narcissism and abuse?* Wisegeek. https://www.wise-geek.com/what-is-the-connection-between-narcissism-and-abuse.htm

Pfeiffer, L. (n.d.). Gaslight | film by Cukor [1944]. In *Encyclopedia Britannica*. Retrieved July 5, 2022 from https://www.britannica.com/topic/Gaslight-film-by-Cukor

Pomerance, M. (n.d.-a). *7 Crucial things no one tells you about recovering from narcissistic abuse*. The Candidly. https://www.thecandidly.com/2019/7-crucial-things-no-one-tells-you-about-recovering-from-narcissistic-abuse

Pomerance, M. (n.d.-b). *This is what narcissistic abuse looks like*. The Candidly.

https://www.thecandidly.com/2019/this-is-what-narcissistic-abuse-looks-like

Quintana, S. (2019, November 12). *What emotional freedom from a narcissist looks like.* Publishous. https://medium.com/publishous/what-emotional-freedom-from-a-narcissist-looks-like-112ef1fd8470

Quotespedia.org. (n.d.). *Do not let the behavior of others destroy your inner peace. - Dalai Lama.* https://www.quotespedia.org/authors/d/dalai-lama/do-not-let-the-behavior-of-others-destroy-your-inner-peace-dalai-lama/

Raypole, C. (2019, November 21). *Covert narcissist: 10 Signs and symptoms.* Healthline. https://www.healthline.com/health/covert-narcissist

Raypole, C. (2020, March 30). *Recovery from narcissistic abuse is possible — here's how.* Healthline. https://www.healthline.com/health/mental-health/9-tips-for-narcissistic-abuse-recovery

Rhodewalt, F. (2019). Narcissistic pathology and behaviour. In *Encyclopædia Britannica.* Retrieved July 5, 2022 from https://www.britannica.com/science/narcissism/Narcissistic-pathology-and-behaviour

Rice, M. (2022, February 7). *What is narcissistic gaslighting?* Talkspace.

https://www.talkspace.com/blog/narcissistic-gas-lighting/

Saxena, S. (2021, November 18). *What is a narcissistic abuse cycle & how does it work?* Choosing Therapy. https://www.choosingtherapy.com/narcissistic-abuse-cycle/

Schneider, A. (2018, June 20). *4 Ways to find peace after a toxic relationship.* Psych Central. https://psychcentral.com/blog/savvy-shrink/2018/06/4-ways-to-find-peace-after-a-toxic-relationship

Scott, E. (2021, January 9). *How to create truly supportive friendships for stress relief.* Verywell Mind. https://www.verywellmind.com/how-to-create-social-support-in-your-life-3144955

Segal, J., Kemp, G., & Smith, M. (2018, November 2). *Dealing with a breakup or divorce.* Helpguide. https://www.helpguide.org/articles/grief/dealing-with-a-breakup-or-divorce.htm

Shafir, H. (2022, June 24). *Narcissist gaslighting: What it is, signs, & how to cope.* Choosing Therapy. https://www.choosingtherapy.com/narcissist-gaslighting/

Smith, E.-M. (2017, September 26). *What are the signs your verbal abuser is a narcissist?* HealthyPlace. https://www.healthyplace.com/blogs/verbalab

useinrelationships/2017/09/are-all-verbal-abusers-narcissists

Smith, M., & Robinson, L. (2021, October). *Narcissistic personality disorder.* HelpGuide. https://www.helpguide.org/articles/mental-disorders/narcissistic-personality-disorder.htm

Smith, S. (2022, February 7). *How to get closure with a narcissist: 12 Ways.* Marriage.com. https://www.marriage.com/advice/mental-health/getting-closure-with-narcissist/

Staff Writers. (2021, April 28). *5 Characteristics of a narcissist.* Best Counseling Degrees. https://www.bestcounselingdegrees.net/resources/characteristics-of-narcissists/

Sullivan, E. J. (2018, July 17). *7 Consequences of verbal abuse.* HealthyPlace. https://www.healthyplace.com/blogs/verbalabuseinrelationships/2018/7/7-consequences-of-verbal-abuse

Taylor, J. (2021, August 23). *3 Essential human freedoms.* Psychology Today. https://www.psychologytoday.com/us/blog/the-power-prime/202108/3-essential-human-freedoms

Team Tony. (n.d.). *How to be more decisive, 7 tips to improve your decision-making skills.* Tony Robbins.

https://www.tonyrobbins.com/stories/unleash-the-power/be-decisive/

The Recovery Village. (2021, August 25). *Narcissistic personality disorder statistics*. The Recovery Village Drug and Alcohol Rehab. https://www.therecoveryvillage.com/mental-health/narcissistic-personality-disorder/npd-statistics/

The Recovery Village. (2022, May 26). *Narcissistic Personality Disorder Myths*. The Recovery Village Drug and Alcohol Rehab. https://www.therecoveryvillage.com/mental-health/narcissistic-personality-disorder/npd-myths/

Thomas, N. (2022, June 21). *Narcissistic abuse: Signs, effects, & treatments*. Choosing Therapy. https://www.choosingtherapy.com/narcissistic-abuse/

Thompson, D. (2015, December 23). *Education for peace: Top 10 ways education promotes peace*. Central Asia Institute. https://centralasiainstitute.org/top-10-ways-education-promotes-peace/

Ward, D. (2012, September 18). *Acceptance is key to dealing with A narcissist*. Psychology Today. https://www.psychologytoday.com/us/blog/sense-and-sensitivity/201209/acceptance-is-key-dealing-narcissist

Washington State Department of Social and Health Services. (n.d.). *Types and signs of abuse.* https://www.dshs.wa.gov/altsa/home-and-community-services/types-and-signs-abuse

Weiss, K. (2021, November 10). *How to get closure from a narcissist.* Kenny Weiss. https://kennyweiss.net/how-to-get-closure-from-a-narcissist-2/

Wiley, C. (2020, March 3). *Is there a difference between narcissism and confidence?* Talkspace. https://www.talkspace.com/blog/narcissist-narcissism-confidence-definition-what-is/

Winsper, C., Bilgin, A., Thompson, A., Marwaha, S., Chanen, A. M., Singh, S. P., Wang, A., & Furtado, V. (2019). The prevalence of personality disorders in the community: a global systematic review and meta-analysis. *The British Journal of Psychiatry, 216*(2), 1–10. https://doi.org/10.1192/bjp.2019.166

WomensLaw.org. (2021, September 8). *Emotional and psychological abuse.* https://www.womenslaw.org/about-abuse/forms-abuse/emotional-and-psychological-abuse

Wood, L. (2018, February 9). *5 Myths about narcissists.* Freedom K9 Project. https://www.freedomk9project.com/single-post/2018/02/10/5-myths-about-narcissists

Wozny, C. (2021, November 25). *Physical complications of verbal abuse.* HealthyPlace. https://www.healthyplace.com/blogs/verbalabuseinrelationships/2021/11/physical-complications-of-verbal-abuse

Manufactured by Amazon.ca
Acheson, AB